# CACTUS
## GUIDE

### LADISLAUS CUTAK

**VAN NOSTRAND REINHOLD COMPANY**
NEW YORK   CINCINNATI   ATLANTA   DALLAS   SAN FRANCISCO
LONDON   TORONTO   MELBOURNE

Copyright © 1956 by Litton Educational Publishing, Inc.
Library of Congress Catalog Card Number 56-8392
ISBN 0-442-21819-2

Published in 1976 by Van Nostrand Reinhold Company
A Division of Litton Educational Publishing, Inc.
450 West 33rd Street
New York, NY 10001

Van Nostrand Reinhold Limited
1410 Birchmount Road
Scarborough, Ontario MIP 2E7, Canada

Van Nostrand Reinhold Australia Pty. Ltd.
17 Queen Street
Mitcham, Victoria 3132, Australia

Van Nostrand Reinhold Company Ltd.
Molly Millars Lane
Workingham, Berkshire, England

16 15 14 13 12 11 10 9 8 7 6 5 4 3 2 1

# *FOREWORD*

I**T IS NOT ESSENTIAL** to live in a desert country to enjoy the cacti—the most bizarre of desert plants that God created. Far more people cultivate the cactus in temperate climes than is imagined. The plants hold a certain fascination; for some it is the strange shapes the cacti assume; for others it is the delicate beauty of the exquisite flowers; and for still others it is the ease with which they can be grown in the home. Most of us are not born to love cacti, but once the bug bites us its sting usually lasts for all time.

I was born far from any desert region; but when my father first brought home a golden spined barrel cactus, a craving for more of its kind possessed me. It left an indelible mark in my heart. It was not until 1927, however, that I realized what part cactus plants would play in my later life and what enjoyment they would bring me. It was then that I started working in the famous Missouri Botanical Garden where a fine collection of cacti was maintained. I was given an opportunity to work with the plants under my father's tutelage. Soon I was making cuttings, propagating by seed, and even grafting the plants.

The desire to learn more led me to read books on the subject, but there weren't too many books written in English about them. Diligently I made my own observations, jotted down notes, acquired a camera to record the habits and flowering of the cacti, and even deviated from the usual methods of growing these bizarre plants just to see how they would respond. In order to be with the plants day and night, I utilized every available window in our modest home for growing them. I also began visiting other collections, made trips to the native haunts of the cacti, and made friends with all the commercial dealers throughout the country.

This book, modest in scope as it must be, then, is written with the hope that it will bring some information to the reader who will aspire to be, or already is, a cactus fan. It is impossible to cram into these pages everything that has been learned about cactus plants, whether culturally or taxonomically, for there are nearly two thousand species listed and various specialists have their own ideas about how to grow them and as to what names should be ascribed to them. This book, I hope, will tell in simple style the fundamental principles that are to be followed in order to grow successfully and enjoy, as I earlier said, "the most bizarre plants that God created."

LADISLAUS CUTAK

*Missouri Botanical Garden*
*St. Louis, Missouri*

# CONTENTS

# LIST OF ILLUSTRATIONS

CHAPTER I

# WHAT IS A CACTUS?

C ACTI ARE perhaps the oddest and most whimsical of all plants. The word *Cactus* is of Greek origin and was applied to a spiny plant of the ancient Hellenic lands. Linnaeus, the father of systematic botany, first established the name to include the few species of the family then known to science. There are two kinds of cacti —those inhabiting desert regions and those living in the jungles. The curious and varied forms of the desert kind are the result of a frugal diet which the arid, sun-scorched desert offers to such plants that tend to live in it. Without a doubt, these are the best examples of desert plant adaptation. On the other hand, the jungle kind are less quaint in appearance, and these usually are epiphytic in habit. Furthermore, they are mostly spineless or, when they do possess spines, these organs are inconspicuous unlike the spiny armament of the desert cacti.

The succulent spurges of the African deserts mimic the desert cacti, but even these African plants cannot boast such utterly fantastic shapes as prevail in the cactus family, which is considered in its entirety as All-American. For Brobdingnagian proportions and Lilliputian dimensions, for fantastic shapes and grotesque forms, the cacti have no equals. Out of these very forbidding, obstinate cactus bodies spring surprisingly beautiful flowers in shades of yellow, scarlet, rose, crimson, purple, violet, and blue. In the case of the night-blooming kinds, the blossoms are often waxy white, sometimes delicately suffused with pink or lightly tinged with green or bronze.

Even though the jungle cacti do not look anything like our popular conception of typical cactus, they do possess characteristics which readily identify them as members of the cactus family. To be a cactus, a plant must possess several distinguishing features not found in other plant families. A cactus can be defined as a perennial plant with various degrees of succulency in its stem, mostly spiny, characterized by specialized organs known as *areoles* and, in addition, must possess certain modifications in the flower and fruit structures—all of which will be defined briefly and simply for a better understanding.

In order for a plant to be a cactus it first must be dicotyledonous, meaning that it produces two seed leaves upon germination; second, it must be perennial, meaning that it lives year after year; third, it must possess areoles, which, as the name implies, are small areas marked out upon the surface of a joint and spaced in regular or irregular fashion; fourth, it has to have an inferior ovary, meaning that the sepals and petals are inserted above the ovary; and fifth, the fruit is a berry, with all the seeds enclosed in one compartment and not divided into sections as in the orange.

The most distinguishing feature of the cactus is the areole which corresponds to nodes on other plants from which leaves, branches, and flowers emerge. Areoles are usually round and consist of two buds; but they can be of other shapes, from minute to fairly large. The pair of buds are often set close together or superimposed, but sometimes, as in Mammillaria, one of the buds will be found in the axil of the tubercle and the other will be located at the tip of it. Usually the areoles are filled with felt, wool, bristles, hair, or spines; occasionally they are naked.

The fascinating Cactus family is best divided into three distinct groups known as tribes, which are subdivided into subtribes, genera, subgenera, species, and varieties. The members of each division have not only the characteristics of the family, but they also have other features in common which set them apart from the rest of the family. A truly studious, enthu-

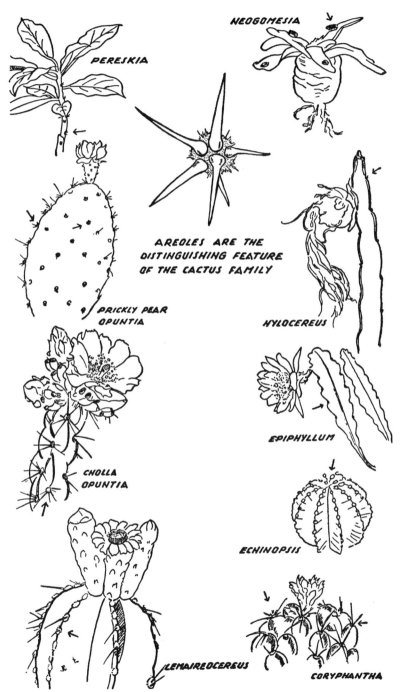

NEOGOMESIA

PERESKIA

AREOLES ARE THE
DISTINGUISHING FEATURE
OF THE CACTUS FAMILY

HYLOCEREUS

PRICKLY PEAR
OPUNTIA

EPIPHYLLUM

CHOLLA
OPUNTIA

ECHINOPSIS

LEMAIREOCEREUS

CORYPHANTHA

3

siastic cactus grower can, in time, learn to distinguish the many forms
contained in the family, but it will not always be an easy task. Fruit and
floral characters play an important role in classification since these organs
are less likely to change than the vegetative portions.

The magnificent opus by Britton and Rose, who gave us a four-volume
treatise on the Cactus family in the English language thirty years ago,
has stirred up quite a controversy in recent years, but their piece of work
is still hailed as the Cactus Bible by botanist and amateur alike. Their
publication, *The Cactaceae,* is now being altered, revised, and torn to
pieces by present-day taxonomists in the light of new discoveries and research, but it still remains the basis for classification of this remarkable
family.

For convenience, Britton and Rose divided the Cactus family into three
major groups or tribes. Each of these tribes has something that neither
of the other two groups has. This is the first step undertaken for the
better understanding of the diverse family.

The first of the three tribes universally recognized is PERESKIEAE or
Pereskia tribe. Members of this group are assumed to be the most primitive of the cacti. For the most part they are woody and leafy trees, shrubs,
and vines which do not resemble in the least any cactus of our imagina-
tion. Many of the arborescent Pereskias might easily be mistaken for
lemon or apple trees. However, since they bear areoles from which spines,
branches, and leaves arise, they are *true* cacti and nothing else. All the
Pereskias bear leaves—large leaves to be sure—which persist on the plant
all year round except those that become deciduous in the dormant season.
No other cactus tribe can boast this feature. The foliage of Pereskias is
mostly nonsucculent, deciduous, or permanent, and therefore this group
should be easily recognizable by even the neophyte. In addition, the
flowers of the Pereskias are stalked and often grow in clusters. In the
other two tribes the flowers are sessile, which means that they are without
a footstalk of any kind.

The second tribe, OPUNTIEAE, best displays the evolutionary trend from
the preceding group which can very easily be followed in its eight or
nine genera. Glochids are the distinguishing feature of the second tribe.
These are tiny barbed bristles which fill the areoles and cause so much
discomfort to the person handling the plants. These glochids or bundles

PERMANENT OR DECIDUOUS
FOLIAGE AND STALKED FLOWERS,
USUALLY IN CLUSTERS.

## PROMINENT CHARACTERS IN PERESKIA TRIBE

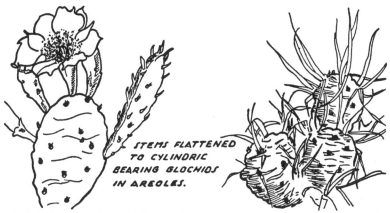

STEMS FLATTENED
TO CYLINDRIC
BEARING GLOCHIDS
IN AREOLES.

## PROMINENT CHARACTERS IN OPUNTIA TRIBE

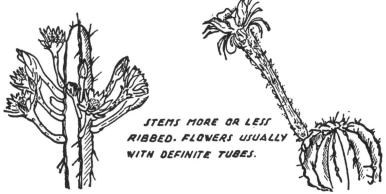

STEMS MORE OR LESS
RIBBED. FLOWERS USUALLY
WITH DEFINITE TUBES.

## PROMINENT CHARACTERS IN CEREUS TRIBE

of tiny spines are easily dislodged from the plant but withdrawn with difficulty from flesh and clothing coming in contact with them. Members of the Opuntia tribe bear minute leaves which soon fall. However, the glochids are the important character to look for to separate this tribe from the other two.

The third tribe, CEREEAE, is the largest of the three. It is most complex in its entirety, and the plants range from the dwarf to the gigantic. There are no glochids in the areoles of the Cereus tribe, no leaves (except in the cotyledonary stage), and no sheathed or barbed spines. The flowers, as a rule, possess definite tubes. More than one hundred genera are included in this tribe and possibly over a thousand species. The showiest and most brilliantly colored flowers grow from the highly succulent stems. Many bloom for only a few days, some for only one night, and a few for an hour or two. Most of the members of the Cereus tribe can also be easily recognized by the more or less prominent ribs which the other two tribes never display.

The above tribes are divided into still smaller groups referred as genera, and each genus is composed of individuals designated as species. To define satisfactorily all the genera in a technical way would entail many pages of expounding and really would serve no useful purpose in this book, so it seems wiser to refer the matter to a number of excellent monographs written on the classification of cacti in the English language. I might add that cactus taxonomy has been undergoing alteration and revision since Britton and Rose published their *Cactaceae* due, no doubt, to new light being shed on extensive research and to new discoveries; but the fact also remains that taxonomists do not always agree on the same names. If the reader wishes to be further enlightened on genera and species, please refer to the following monographs:

*The Cactaceae*, by N. L. Britton and J. N. Rose, 1919-1923. Carnegie Institution of Washington Publication No. 248.
*Cactaceae*, by W. Taylor Marshall and Thor Methven Bock, 1941.
*The Mammillaria Handbook*, by Robert T. Craig, 1945.
*Cacti*, by J. Borg, 1937. Revised Edition, 1951.

CHAPTER II

# VARIETIES OF CACTI

THERE ARE nearly two thousand species and varieties of cactus plants, but it would be impossible to describe all of them, even briefly, in a book of this size. I will attempt to acquaint you with as many of the night-blooming kinds as possible, as well as the fascinating pincushions and the epiphytic types, but there are several other interesting groups which demand attention in order to round out a near complete survey of the family.

The Pereskias, considered to be the most primitive of cacti, generally are not cultivated to a great extent because they demand lots of room for proper development since they are vigorous bushes, trees, and vines. However, some species should be cultivated because they are ornamental as well as useful for grafting stock. Zygocactus, Schlumbergera, and Rhipsalis are most ideal to graft on Pereskias. Also the long spines produced on certain Pereskias are excellent for holding grafts in place. Pereskias flower readily even on small cuttings.

The Pereskia group is the only cactus group bearing permanent foliage. In some cases, the leaves drop off during the period of rest. Probably the oldest species in cultivation is *Pereskia aculeata,* a climbing or rampant shrub most frequently employed in grafting. The blossoms are produced in large clusters and are strongly lemon-scented. *Pereskia sacharosa* probably bears the largest flower, which in form and color looks like a big single rose. The best, in my estimation, for pot culture is *Pereskia corrugata*. Its foliage is bright green, crinkled in appearance, and produces rich scarlet-orange blossoms at the tips of the branches. It is a collector's item at present, but several California nurseries have it in stock and it should be available to the trade soon. Cuttings will root even in water. All Pereskias are easy to grow and require more water than the true desert kinds.

The Opuntia group is interesting and a few species are regularly used in dish gardening. However, this group bears glochids (tiny cushions of spines) in the areoles, and improper handling of the plants may cause discomfort to a person. For this reason I usually do not recommend these plants for the beginner. Yet, I must admit that a number of species are very attractive and less likely to irritate skin. As a precaution, handle these plants with a pair of tweezers or ice tongs.

The best known members in this group are the Opuntias, which can be divided into the Prickly Pears and the Chollas. Prickly Pears are distinguished by their pad-like joints and mostly edible fruits; the Chollas by cylindrical stems and dry fruit. The latter are often arborescent, and their woody skeletons are sought by novelty seekers to be used in making cactus wood furniture, picture frames, plant containers, etc. All the Opuntias are fairly easy to grow. Each joint or portion of a joint falling to the ground strikes root easily. Keep Opuntias on the dry side, especially in the winter season.

Only a few of the best species will be mentioned for your consideration. I like *Opuntia brasiliensis* very much. It produces a tree-like stem and bears spreading side branches with rather thin flat joints. The glochids and few spines are not troublesome. *Opuntia monacantha* is another worthwhile species, especially the variegated form which is beautifully marbled in white, yellow, and even pink. A near spineless species is *Opuntia elata*. The pads are small, quite thick, and of an olive-green color with flowers of orange hue. The most common one for dishes and novelty containers is *Opuntia microdasys,* called Bunny Ears or Velvet Cactus. The small joints are spineless but punctuated with prominent areoles filled with glochids of golden yellow, and, in some forms, white, brown, or red. *Opuntia orbiculata* in youth bears long, curly, white hair which makes it deservedly popular. Still another white-haired species is *Opuntia vestita.*

In the Cholla group the most popular seems to be the Boxing Glove, a crested form of *Opuntia fulgida.* The tips of the small cylindric joints split and grow fanwise, often resembling boxing gloves—hence the common name. *Opuntia vilis* is a well branched, tiny tree which the florists use in dish gardens. It is only two to three inches tall. In the same class is *Opuntia Verschaffeltii,* which has a low spreading habit, and purplish tinged joints when exposed to sunlight. A curious oddity is *Opuntia strobiliformis* which is spineless, but still possesses the glochids, which in this case, are deeply embedded so that the plant can be handled easily. The joints resemble a pine or spruce cone. Still another oddity which should be included in every cactus fancier's collection is *Opuntia glomerata.* It is of quicker growth than the preceding but requires the same treatment—a sunny location, sandy soil, and moderate waterings in summer. The joints are short and globose, covered with low, broad warts on which are situated the prominent areoles displaying long, papery-white ribbons that serve as spines. Opuntia pads and cylindric joints can effectively be used in floral arrangements, as Mrs. Sophia Becker has demonstrated in all the shows sponsored by the Henry Shaw Cactus Society.

## HEDGEHOGS AND BARREL CACTI

The Echinocereus group contains very spiny plants to which the common name Hedgehog is often applied. The flowers of all members are fairly large and usually highly colored. The plants are low, erect or prostrate, and often grow in huge clumps or colonies. In Texas and other Southwestern States some species possess a hundred or more heads to a cluster. The group is difficult to identify because so-called old species intergrade with each other and at best are only geographical variants of a few type species. *Echinocereus Reichenbachii* at one time flooded the dime store market. This is the plant known as Lace Cactus because the spines form an intricate lacy cover for the plant body. *Echinocereus rigidissimus* is another form found in collections and is the popular Rainbow Cactus, so named because of the alternate zones of white, pink, red, or brown spines that cover the plant. Echinocerei are all North American, but they have their counterparts in South America in the genus Echinopsis, commonly referred to as Easter Lily Cactus. Plants in this genus are among the most satisfactory because they are easy to grow and have handsome blooms. The globular to columnar stems are heavily ribbed and spined in most species, and they produce an abundance of offsets or "pups" over the entire plant which can be easily dislodged and grown individually. These pups are excellent for spoon gardens, dish gardens, strawberry jars, and small novelty containers.

*Echinopsis Eyriesii* has long been a favorite with home gardeners. It is a globular to almost cylindrical cactus with prominent, deeply furrowed ribs. Flowers appear on the sides in late afternoon and are white, trumpet-shaped, and about ten inches long. *Echinopsis multiplex* is a free flowering species and highly desirable because of its fragrant, pink flowers. A dull green, globular cactus with a much shorter flower is *Echinopsis Kratochviliana* from Northern Argentina. It is an excellent dwarf subject for the kitchen window.

Closely allied to Echinocereus and Echinopsis are Rebutias and Lobivias. Rebutias are mostly small plants which resemble Mammillarias; and, although they do not offer any great diversity of form, they are excellent for one who has limited space. I call them the Tom Thumbs of the cactus world. Their flowers are small, ranging in color from deep red to orange, and last for several days. The Lobivias, on the other hand, are much larger plants with larger flowers. There must be at least seventy or eighty species and many horticultural hybrids, the latter more free-flowering and with finer shades of color. The standard flower color is red, but yellow and white are also found. *Lobivia aurea* has lovely yellow blossoms on the order of Echinopsis. *Lobivia famatimensis* is one of the finest flowering; and *Lobivia huascha,* in appearance and habit, looks more like a Trichocereus. It bears both golden yellow and rich red blossoms.

One of the most popular of dwarf cacti is the Peanut Cactus, *Chamaecereus Silvestrii.* The joints, which are small and about the thickness of a peanut, drop off at the least touch. An abundance of red, diurnal flowers are produced on the stems. During the growing period Chamae-

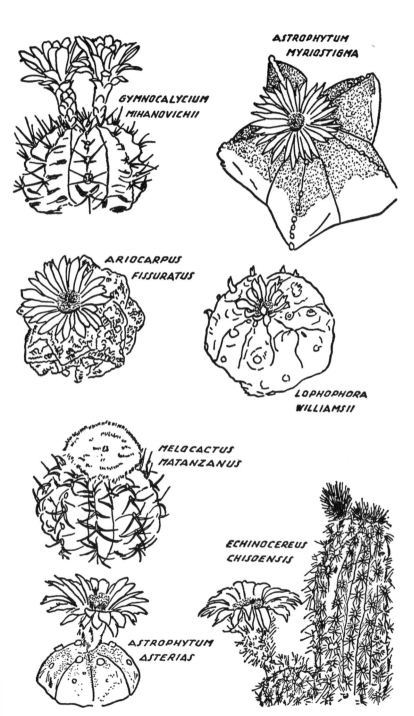

GYMNOCALYCIUM
MIHANOVICHII

ASTROPHYTUM
MYRIOSTIGMA

ARIOCARPUS
FISSURATUS

LOPHOPHORA
WILLIAMSII

MELOCACTUS
MATANZANUS

ECHINOCEREUS
CHISOENSIS

ASTROPHYTUM
ASTERIAS

II

cereus loves frequent watering. Give the plant full sun. When grafted onto a Cereus it soon produces a globose head of joints.

The fascinatingly interesting Barrel Cactus group (Echinocactanae) contains plants with a globular type of stem, which can be extremely large or decidedly small, simple or clustered, and very spiny or without any spines at all. Many collector's items can be found in this group, including Living Rocks, Bishop Caps, Chin Cacti, Silver and Golden Balls, and Barrels, to name a few. *Ariocarpus fissuratus* is a curious plant with horny, fissured, triangular tubercles arranged in a rosette. Growing among rocks in its native Texas and Mexico, it is indistinguishable from the surrounding stones. When the dainty pink flowers appear in August from among the horny tubercles, the plant literally becomes a Living Rock. There are several other species available in the trade. *Aztekium Ritteri, Obregonia Denegri, Encephalocarpus strobiliformis* and the few species in genus Strombocactus all can be classed as Living Rocks because of their mimicry.

The well known Bishop Cap, *Astrophytum myriostigma,* should be in every collection as it is easy to grow, flowers when small, and needs very little care. It is entirely spineless, the plant body, stone-like in appearance, usually possessing four or five very prominent broad ribs and densely dotted with white specks. The Sand Dollar, *Astrophytum asterias,* has a flat, dome-shaped body divided into eight broad, rounded ribs, each one punctuated by a row of small white woolly areoles, and likewise is entirely spineless. *Astrophytum ornatum,* sometimes called Star Cactus, is another oddity beautifully flecked with star-like, silvery scales. All the Astrophytums require a porous sandy or rocky soil, rich in lime, lots of sunlight, and frequent watering in the summer when they make their best growth. They must be kept more or less dry in winter.

A curiosity is the Dumpling Cactus, *Lophophora Williamsii,* which should be in every collection. This is the famous Peyote of Mexico used in religious rituals because of its narcotic properties. The plant has a long and thick taproot and a round, soft, spineless top divided into broad, flattened ribs which bear a series of low tubercles prominent with a tuft of matted hairs. It prefers lots of sunshine, sandy soil, and moderate waterings.

Gymnocalyciums are extremely interesting cacti, easily grown and easily flowered. They are all globular plants characterized by a more or less pronounced protuberance or "chin" below the areoles—hence their common name. They love a moderately rich and porous soil, with plenty of water when growing, and a sunny position. More than fifty species are recognized, *Gymnocalycium Mihanovichii* being a universal favorite. It is a small banded cactus with a chartreuse flower appearing in spring and continuing until fall.

Notocactus and Malacocarpus are mostly globular to short, cylindric, simple or clustered cacti that bear their flowers from the top and are freely produced. They all have fibrous roots and can stand considerable water during the summer as long as good, well drained soil is supplied. The flowers are mostly yellow to orange with a red stigma. *Notocactus Leninghausii* is a very desirable species because the cylindric stem is thickly clothed with soft, flexible, hair-like golden spines.

Don't overlook the Parodias. They constitute a very satisfactory group, consisting of small globular plants that somewhat resemble Mammillarias and often are bright spined. The fairly large flowers are borne on the new areoles at the top of the plant and are golden yellow, orange red, fiery scarlet, glossy carmine, and even white. Parodias will do well in the window. Like most cacti, they are more likely to be killed by kindness than by neglect.

Echinofossulocactus is a distinct genus comprising rather small plants with numerous thin, often wavy, ribs. The common name, Brain Cactus, is often applied to them. Flowers are quite pretty in various shades of pink, yellow, green, white, and blue. They like to be kept on the dry side, especially in winter. Water when dry but never saturate them.

Members of genera Echinocactus and Ferocactus are the true Barrel Cactus. When young, the plants are globular, but in age they become tall and cylindric, often five or more feet high. Usually they are viciously armed with stout spines of varied hue. The best known is the Golden Ball, *Echinocactus Grusonii,* a most beautiful species with golden spines that glisten in the sun. Seedlings are very attractive, and the species is a slow grower—specimens two to four feet tall and round as a barrel may be twenty-five to one hundred years old. *Ferocactus Wislizenii* is probably the best known in its particular group. Sometimes called Fishhook Cactus, it dots the landscape in Southern Arizona and extends as far as

El Paso, Texas. More than thirty other species are recognized, and all are worthy of cultivation.

The Turk's Cap Cactus, *Melocactus intortus,* is one of the most whimsical of all cacti. The plant body is melon-shaped and develops a cephalium or head at the top of the plant. This cephalium is covered with bristles and hairs and produces tiny flowers. In *Melocactus intortus* the cephalium is sometimes as long as the plant body; and, since it resembles a Turk's fez, it receives its picturesque name from it. Melocacti are natives of tropical regions of the West Indies, Mexico, Central America, and South America and have to be grown in full sun and kept comparatively dry, lest too much water will start a rot condition.

## PINCUSHION CACTI

### MAMMILLARIAS

To many amateur cactus fans, the Mammillarias are probably the darlings of the whole cactus family. Its members are, for the most part, small plants with simple or often clustered cylindrical to globular bodies, conspicuously covered with numerous mammillae or nipples, from whence the generic name is derived. These nipples or tubercles are capped with areoles from which spring forth delicate or strong spines of various sizes. The flowers, however, do not arise from the areole proper but are rather borne from the usually hairy or woolly axils of the old tubercles near the top of the plants. The flowers, comparatively small and more or less bell-shaped, make up for their diminutive size by being produced in abundance in the form of dazzling crowns in red, pink, white, yellow, and purple. The beauty of the plants is further enhanced by the colorful clavate fruits, which in some species appear at the same time as the flowers.

The genus Mammillaria is predominantly Mexican, where at least two hundred species have been discovered and where perhaps many more are yet to be located. In most instances they prefer the more arid sections, but occasionally they are found thriving in the damper climates of lower altitudes. Although terrestrial in habit, on rare occasions they may find abode in trees or better still in crevices of precipitous canyon walls. In Oaxaca I spotted pincushion cacti growing in the middle of clumping orchids on rock faces. The distribution of Mammillarias extends as far north as Oklahoma, New Mexico, Arizona, and California and as far south as Colombia and Venezuela in South America. The species are scarce in the West Indies, Central America, and coastal islands.

Although Mammillarias grow over most of Mexico, the most conspicuous masses in evidence are in the central plateau region. Beautiful clusters of *Mammillaria compressa* can be viewed in the neighborhood of Ixmiquilpan, Zimapan, and Actopan not far from the highway. This is not the only common species in evidence; there are dozens of others producing clusters of many heads. A second distributional area is located in northwest Mexico, particularly in Sonora and Chihuahua, where scores of pincushions dot the mountainous terrain. It is here that many more varieties will be found as inroads are made to the inaccessible hostile mountain retreats. The third distributional area is the fascinating peninsula of Baja California with its adjacent islands. Explorations there have uncovered many peculiar plants characteristic to no other location on the mainland.

The cultivation of Mammillarias is by no means difficult. Single mature specimens are usually adaptable for the four-inch flower pot. The soil, on the whole, must not be as rich in humus as that given to the Epiphyllums, but rather made up of thoroughly decomposed leaf soil or sod mixed with at least the same quantity of sand. Crushed limestone is advisable for the mixture. To make the soil more porous, I frequently use a generous supply of gravel. Mammillarias require water, especially during the growing season; but during the winter months they ought to be kept quite dry and held in a dormant state in cool, well lit places.

Mammillarias possess an appeal likened to no other cactus. Since they are so diverse in form of body and spine armament, one could easily prefer a collection of them alone and get as much satisfaction out of them as another would with a more complete assortment of cacti and succulents. One real advantage not to be overlooked is that Mammillarias do not take up much room. Some species are very free-flowering and may bloom from seed within a year or two. Fifteen-month-old seedling *Mammillaria bocasana* owned by one of our local cactus growers was blooming profusely. Pincushion cacti like to be confined in smaller containers and therefore are excellent subjects for novelty pottery. Grafted to some stout stock of Cereus, Lemaireocereus, and Trichocereus, they will produce excellent heads in a short time.

Since there are so many kinds of Mammillarias, the easiest way to understand them is to divide them into three groups—namely, those having milky sap, those with semi-milky sap, and those with watery sap. Whenever I attempt to identify a strange Mammillaria, the first thing I do is to prick it with a pin or needle to determine the type of sap it possesses. Usually one prick into a tubercle or nipple will disclose the kind of sap present. This prick need not be too deep or conspicuous. No harm will come to the plant because the sap coagulates readily and heals over the cut. Nearly one hundred species of Mammillaria possess milky sap, and strangely only the forms with straight central spines are involved. The semi-milky sap is usually characteristic to plants producing brown seeds. There are only about ten species in this class. The remainder, more than a hundred and fifty species, have watery sap which is usually associated with all the plants possessing hooked central spines. However, it is to be remembered that there are slight exceptions in all three groups.

After one is certain about the sap content, the next step toward identification of species is to count the tubercle arrangement which comes in spiral rows, in both clockwise and counterclockwise directions. This spiral arrangement is fairly consistent throughout the genus. However, one must train himself to be able to count the spirals as they are not always prominent, especially when wool, hair, and spines nearly obscure them. In some strange, unexplainable manner the spirals usually occur in a precise mathematical series of 3 and 5, 5 and 8, 8 and 13, 13 and 21, 21 and 34, and 34 and 55. Mr. E. Shurly, British expert on the Mammillarias, states that this definitely points to a relation between tubercles and leaves of normal plants. Mr. Shurly also points out that roots and the type of body growth are definite and stable characteristics of Mammillarias and aid in their identification. Mammillarias have either taproots or non-taproots. The taproots vary in shape from the elongated, carrot type to a molar tooth-shape. The growths are divided into simple, cespitose, twin, and dichotomous. Simple growth means that a plant remains single and does not reproduce by offshoots. Cespitose denotes a clustered habit. Twin or finger growth indicates the type where basal offshoots grow as long as the mother plant and appear like a bunch of fingers upraised. Dichotomous means that a plant head divides in two, without becoming separate plants.

Since it would be practically impossible to describe in this book all the known Mammillarias, the next best thing is to acquaint you with some of the more outstanding kinds. The species with milky sap will be discussed first.

*Mammillaria compressa* is one of the nicest pincushions in existence. It forms beautiful clusters up to three feet broad and is very abundant in the neighborhood of Zimapan and Ixmiquilpan, interesting old towns colonized by the Spanish more than four centuries ago. When one views these huge clumps in nature in Old Mexico or in outdoor rockeries in California, it is certainly a sight long to be remembered. Sometimes single mounds may consist of several hundred individual heads. The closely set nipples are firm in texture and dense white wool appears in their axils, particularly in the newer ones at the crown which give it a characteristic appearance. The spines, all radial and very unequal, are variable in length, sometimes nearly four inches long. Deep purplish-pink flowers appear in March followed later by bright red fruits.

*Mammillaria magnimamma* is another very conspicuous and common pincushion which is abundant on the central plateau, where it forms large mounds but never as high as in *Mammillaria compressa*. The individual heads are rather deep-seated so as to be almost level with the ground. In the Pedregal near Mexico City this pincushion is rather common, but it blends so perfectly with the lava rock that the clusters can easily be overlooked. This species also grows on a hillside outside of Mexico City, which incidentally is the most sacred spot in Mexico, being the place of the miraculous appearance of the Virgin of Guadalupe. The pincushion is also variable in its spine arrangement. The flowers are a dirty cream color.

*Mammillaria confusa* is another variable species which includes three varieties, all found in Oaxaca within a twenty-five-mile radius of the capital city. Abundant wool and tortuous white bristles appear in the axils, and the flowers are pale greenish, making their appearance in early spring and continuing into fall.

*Mammillaria Karwinskiana* is a robust grower with a variable spine arrangement, all spines heavy, needle-like, nearly straight to slightly recurved, and with cream-colored blossoms.

*Mammillaria Collinsii* is a closely allied species which I collected in Oaxaca, where it formed small clusters. White wool and tortuous bristles in the axils of the tubercles and more spines are prominent in the areoles in addition to a central which is slightly stouter but practically identical in color.

*Mammillaria nejapensis* is another interesting pincushion which I collected in Oaxaca in the vicinity of Nejapa, from which location it received its specific name. It possesses many, very long and tortuous axillary bristles which nearly hide the tubercles. There is a form with very short spines and another with much longer ones.

*Mammillaria uncinata* is one of the few milk-bearing Mammillarias having hooked spines. The central spine is usually solitary and much stouter than the radials.

*Mammillaria carnea* was first described in 1837 and is a globose to cylindric cactus with angular tubercles supporting only central spines in its areoles. The pink blossoms are rather small but form a colorful ring at the top.

*Mammillaria mystax* is another "old timer" characterized by long, erect, central spines which overtop the plant in the wild state but which are usually lost in cultivation. Dark red flowers later produce red fruit.

*Mammillaria sempervivi* is a rather fascinating pincushion with a depressed apex, crowded short tubercles with abundant wool in their axils, and rather short spines. The dirty white flowers with reddish lines appear

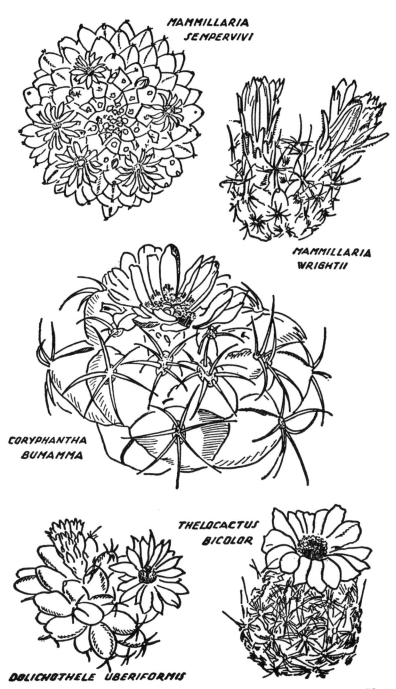

MAMMILLARIA
SEMPERVIVI

MAMMILLARIA
WRIGHTII

CORYPHANTHA
BUMAMMA

THELOCACTUS
BICOLOR

DOLICHOTHELE UBERIFORMIS

near the apex. I found this plant growing on the rocky slopes of a canyon in Hidalgo noted for its spectacular Old Man cacti.

*Mammillaria nivosa* is one of the few pincushions native to the islands of the Caribbean. It is a very spiny cactus characterized by dense, white wool in the axils of the tubercles and, for this reason, is sometimes known as the snowy cactus.

*Mammillaria geminispina* is one of the prettiest of the clustering pincushions, not only for its neat appearance but for the beauty of its dark red flowers. The white wool is very dense in the axils of the upper tubercles and the black tipped central spines are outlined against this background.

*Mammillaria hemisphaerica* is a Texas pincushion which at one time was offered for sale in dime stores all over the country. The plants bloom very early in the spring, beginning in February and ending in April. The cream-colored flowers are about a half inch broad. Sometimes fruits appear at the same time as the flowers but they are from the previous year's blooms. They are bright red and club-shaped.

*Mammillaria applanata* closely resembles the preceding but is more flattened at the top, and *Mammillaria Heyderi,* another near relative, is distinguished by having more radial spines. The last three species are plentiful in Texas.

*Mammillaria Hahniana,* first discovered in 1929, became the most sought-after pincushion because of its cloak of long, white hair. It is aptly dubbed Old Lady Cactus. The purple-red flowers appear in spring and continue to summer, staying open for several days. This one ought to be included in every collection.

*Mammillaria chionocephala* is an elegant plant which I first saw wild in a canyon near Arteaga Falls in northeastern Mexico. The globose plant body is almost hidden by the white spines.

*Mammillaria Parkinsonii* is an interesting pincushion which forms large mounds. Its yellowish-cream flowers are surrounded by a mass of wool. The characteristic feature is the chalky white color of the stout, long, central spines.

In the Mammillaria group featuring watery sap there are several worthwhile species to choose from. *Mammillaria camptotricha,* appropriately named Birdnest Pincushion, produces soft curling, yellow spines and, because of this, can be handled with ease. The plant tends to cluster and has a characteristic deep green color. The tubercles are slender, often cylindrical, and about a half inch long. The whitish flowers are small and set in the nest of spines. It is an easy cactus to grow in semishade or full sun.

*Mammillaria elongata,* the Finger Cactus, is a popular pincushion which branches freely from the base to form handsome specimens. The individual stems, three to four inches high, are slender and cylindrical with short conic tubercles crowned with a diadem of golden star-like spines. It is a variable species and an easy propagator.

*Mammillaria plumosa,* the Featherball Cactus, is a remarkable pincushion which grows in the fissures of calcareous rocks, over which it spreads and binds together, at the same time blending with the limestone so that it is hard to detect. I found it in the vicinity of Ojo Caliente in Coahuila, Mexico. The bodies are globular and are characterized by soft-textured tubercles topped by clusters of radiating, soft, silky, feather-like, white spines. This most lovely species ought to be grown in every collection.

*Mammillaria Schiedeana* is another choice example, likewise soft textured, the short conical tubercles of which are crowned with areoles possessing innumerable, pubescent, golden-yellow spines giving the plant a frilled appearance.

*Mammillaria lasiacantha,* a miniature pincushion, is a globular plant entirely covered with soft spines. Under a hand lens these spines are seen to be pubescent. The cactus, native to Texas and New Mexico, flowers in April and May and has white flowers, each petal marked by a red-purple midstripe. A form without the pubescent spines is called *Mammillaria lasiacantha* var. *denudata.*

*Mammillaria dioica* is extremely variable in body size and coloration of spines but grows in abundance in the coastal area of southern California where I first saw it in the vicinity of San Diego. Flowers appear in a ring around the top and are cream-colored with a fine, purple midstripe.

*Mammillaria pygmaea,* which comes from central Mexico, is a small clustering pincushion that grows rapidly and bears hair-like, white, radial spines completely covering the plant body, but the central spines are golden-yellow which sets them off very nicely.

*Mammillaria zephyranthoides* is a beautiful species that must be kept on the dry side in winter. It is a flattened, globose pincushion with few, large, soft tubercles and quite large creamish flowers with a carmine-red midstripe.

*Mammillaria Blossfeldiana* from Baja California intrigued me the minute I laid eyes on a blooming plant in Gates Cactus Nursery last summer. It tends to be a solitary plant but occasionally clusters from the base. There are about twenty radial spines in each areole and four centrals; the radials are radiating, short, needle-like, yellowish to grayish-white with dark brown to black tips, while the centrals are purplish to black most of the way and one of them is hooked. The rather large funnel-form flowers emerge from near the apex and last for several days. They are carmine-pink and have a darker midline. The green stigma lobes and orange-yellow anthers add distinction.

*Mammillaria bombycina* is a real beauty, being one of the loveliest of all Mammillarias. The stem is globular becoming cylindrical with age and clusters freely at the base. It is extremely woolly at the top so that the tubercles are entirely covered by the immaculate wool. The white radial spines make a fine, lacy pattern over the gray-green plant, whose beauty is further heightened by the lower hooked central spine which is white to amber-yellow in the lower half and brownish-red in the upper half. Flowers come from near the apex and are deep pink with a darker midstripe. Don't overlook this species.

*Mammillaria microcarpa* is mostly a solitary plant, although occasionally it sprouts from both base and body. It is a beautiful fishhook variety. The radial spines are whitish and star-like, almost completely hiding the plant body. One to three centrals are present, and they are red upon emergence turning to dark brown and black, with one of them strongly hooked. The lovely pink blossoms form a ring at the top to make a beautiful picture. In Arizona it is fairly common growing among rock with which it blends perfectly. The plant also grows in Texas, California, and Mexico.

*Mammillaria bocasana,* the Powder Puff, is aptly named, because it is covered by long, white silky hairs which serve as a veil for the short, brown, hooked, central spines beneath the camouflage. It is a lovely and popular species, flowering freely. In fact, it is a jewel among cacti. The yellowish-white flowers have a red midrib and tip.

*Mammillaria Guelzowiana* is closely related to the preceding but it is larger and not as freely clustering. It also has a much larger blossom of deep purplish-red.

*Mammillaria hidalgensis* is one of the taller and more robust pincushions which divides by dichotomous branching. Its tubercles are slenderly conical, tipped with two to four central spines. The flowering crown is quite woolly, the carmine-red flowers making an effective display. Old specimens attain twelve inches or more in height and about five inches in diameter.

*Mammillaria tetracantha* is another large quick growing pincushion, which is spinier, with usually much longer spines and pretty carmine-red blossoms produced from the woolly white axils.

*Mammillaria rhodantha* is extremely variable in spine color and length. Its radials can be white or yellow and the centrals white, yellow, red, or brown. Deep purplish-pink blossoms are produced in a ring near the top. There are many varieties, most of them classified according to color, length, and texture of the spines. This species grows in fertile soil on the central plateau of Mexico and sometimes forms large clumps.

*Mammillaria echinaria* is a very small, desirable plant closely allied to *Mammillaria elongata* but generally distinguished from it by the presence of one or more central spines, which usually are lacking in the latter. It soon forms handsome clusters and produces creamish blossoms with faint salmon midstripe. I found it under bushes near Ixmiquilpan, in Mexico. *Mammillaria Pringlei* is a most beautiful species of striking appearance. It possesses long, golden-yellow spines and crimson blossoms.

*Mammillaria Ortiz-Rubiona* is still another desirable species with cylindrical tubercles. White bristles, longer than the tubercles, issue from their axils, and numerous radial white spines of feathery appearance are in each areole. The four to six centrals are much stouter but also white. Flowers are yellowish-pink, followed by carmine, club-shaped berries.

*Mammillaria spinosissima* is a handsome species with dense spines of bristle-like texture ranging from white to ruby-red. Its stem is solitary, columnar, up to twelve inches high; and the flowers, from the upper part of the plant, are lilac or reddish-pink and faintly fragrant.

*Mammillaria prolifera* is a very free clustering and spreading cactus of small stature, native to the West Indies. The globose to short, cylindric stems are only two inches tall and about an inch in diameter, composed of soft-fleshed tubercles which bear numerous hair-like white radial spines and up to nine pale-yellow centrals in their areoles. The yellow-cream blossoms have the characteristic darker midrib.

*Mammillaria multiceps* is a near relative of the above, found in Texas and Mexico. It is smaller in every part and has yellowish centrals with reddish-brown tips.

*Mammillaria elegans* is a popular pincushion with numerous, small, closely set nipples tipped with chalk-white, bristle-like radial spines and stouter centrals. It is truly an elegant plant, as the specific name implies, and there are several varieties established upon minor characteristics, among these variety *supertexta* being rather outstanding and very free flowering.

### CORYPHANTHA

Now that I have described a number of Mammillarias and you have noticed that they are all usually small plants characterized by odd tubercles or nipples producing their small flowers from the axils of the old tubercles near the top of the plants, we learn of another interesting genus, known as Coryphantha. It is so strikingly similar to Mammillaria that the average cactus fan has difficulty in telling the groups apart. One or two distinguishing remarks will be sufficient to clear this situation. Coryphanthas, on the whole, have larger and showier flowers than the Mammillarias, and these are borne from the base of the young and growing tubercles near the tops of the plants. A more distinguishing feature is the pronounced groove which appears on the upper side of each nipple in a fully matured plant. The nipple groove, however, is not solely characteristic to Coryphantha alone, as it will be found in other closely related genera, such as Escobaria and Neobesseya.

At present there are over sixty species of Coryphantha, and these are distributed solely in the desert and mountain regions of North America, the largest concentration being in Mexico. Our southwestern states have a fair representation but are not comparable to our neighbor below the Rio Grande. One species has invaded Canada, while another claims Cuba for its home. The culture is the same as for Mammillaria, with the stress on perfect drainage.

*Coryphantha vivipara* is the commonest representative in the United States and has been reported from at least a dozen states, all west of the Mississippi River. It is a rather attractive species, particularly when in blossom, and will stand hard freezing in our rockeries, but it must occupy a dry position in such a garden, particularly during the winter season. The nippled stems are globular in shape and densely covered with clusters of radiating spines. The usual number of radial spines is sixteen, and there are one to four centrals. The flowers open in bright sunlight, close for the evening, and repeat this operation for two or three days in succession. The blossoms are purplish-pink with pointed, fringed perianth segments. This spiny pincushion can be found in the sandstone hills around Salina, Kansas, on the plains of eastern Colorado, and in the Arbuckle Mountains of Oklahoma, just in case you want to hunt for them. There are several closely related species of the above which now are generally classified as varieties of it, such as *aggregata, arizonica,* and *deserti.* The first variety grows at elevations of 3,000 to 7,000 feet above sea level in Arizona. In 1935 I had the opportunity to collect this clustered variety in the rocky situations of the Pinal Mountains, above Superior. When they were brought back and established in the Cactus House at Shaw's Garden, they attracted attention because of their similarity to golf balls; hence, they were christened "Golfball Cactus."

*Coryphantha macromeris* is an interesting Texas species and one of the easiest to grow. It is found in the Big Bend country, where it is quite plentiful, if you know where to look for it. It is characterized by extra large, soft and loosely arranged tubercles which are grooved only halfway to the base. The flowers are deep purple and free flowering.

*Coryphantha Runyonii* reminds one of *Coryphantha macromeris,* but its spines are shorter and less numerous, and its tubercles are stumpier. It grows in the lower Rio Grande Valley in southern Texas.

*Coryphantha recurvata* is one of the larger pincushion types from Sonora, Mexico, but it also can be found in southern Arizona. It often grows in clusters of five to fifty densely spiny heads and produces lemon-yellow flowers. As its specific name indicates, its yellowish spines are recurved.

*Coryphantha clava* is a tall growing species that clusters with age. The axils of the tubercles are filled with white wool, with a scarlet gland at the base of the groove. The radial and central spines are both yellow. The pale-yellow blossoms are very large and showy.

*Coryphantha elephantidens* has large flattened tubercles of pale green and woolly areoles which in age become naked. Strong, spreading, curved, brownish spines with black tips are produced in the areoles. The flowers are nearly four inches broad when fully expanded.

*Coryphantha Palmeri* is a small, globular pincushion with black-tipped white or yellowish radials and stoutly hooked centrals. It grows among the rocky debris in Coahuila, and sports pale-yellow blossoms.

*Coryphantha pallida,* another small globular cactus with whitish, appressed radial spines and pale-yellow flowers, grows in the calcareous soil of the Tehuacan desert in southern Mexico.

*Coryphantha robustispina* reaches a height of nearly eight inches with a diameter of four or five inches. It grows singly or in clumps, densely armed and almost hidden by the spines. The tubercles are grayish-green. The flowers are salmon-pink with a yellow tinge.

*Coryphantha bumamma* is an odd, globular pincushion with few, large, rounded tubercles supporting stout recurved spines. It possesses a thick root which anchors the plant securely into the ground. The native habitat is Guerrero.

*Coryphantha ramillosa* is the first cactus species I described in the *Cactus and Succulent Journal* of the Cactus and Succulent Society of America. It was discovered in Reagan Canyon—Big Bend country—in Texas. Definitely it is a distinct plant despite its simulating habits to two or three other species. Its spiny armament greatly resembles a small bundle of dried twigs, from which it receives its specific name. The numerous interlocking grayish spines all but hide the plant body from view. Unlike *Coryphantha macromeris,* to which relationship it belongs, it is decidedly hard and firm in every respect. The flowers are large, showy, very variable, pale pink to deep rose-purple.

### DOLICHOTHELE

A genus very close to Mammillaria and having only a few species is Dolichothele. It means "long nipple," referring to the elongated tubercles which are a characteristic feature. In Mammillaria the tubercles are arranged in a regular series of spiral rows, but in Dolichothele there are no definite spirals noticeable. The flowers are quite large and always yellow.

*Dolichothele longimamma* is the oldest known species, first described in 1828 under Mammillaria. The long, soft, green tubercles are up to two inches long surmounted by small, round areoles bearing nine or ten pubescent, flexuous, white to yellow radial spines and one to three centrals of darker hue.

*Dolichothele uberiformis* has much shorter tubercles with fewer spines and no centrals.

*Dolichothele sphaerica* is a Texas species with butter-yellow flowers which are produced in profusion. The plant clusters heavily and its spines are smooth as distinguished from the soft hairy ones of the two preceding species. Dolichothele has watery sap.

### THELOCACTUS

Thelocactus is another genus of pincushion cacti. The name, coined from the Greek, refers to the nippled ribs which this group exhibits. The best known species is *Thelocactus bicolor* which is abundant even in Texas where I found large colonies in the Big Bend country around Marathon. The plants are simple, ribbed and very spiny, with pretty deep-pink to purple flowers appearing in spring and continuing into fall. The spiny armament is highly colored, and several varieties have been proposed to take care of the variations encountered. In Thelocactus are found several groups of unrelated plants which need more thorough study. One example is *Thelocactus uncinatus,* the Cat's Claw Cactus, which has at one time been placed in the following genera by various authors: Echinocactus, Ferocactus, Hamatocactus, and Echinomastus.

### NEOLLOYDIA

The genus Neolloydia contains only a few species which are rather small with spirally arranged nippled ribs and which bear large flowers on the new areoles at the top. The tubercles are grooved above. One species, *Neolloydia texensis,* is found in Texas, where it forms small clusters. It has white, widely spreading radial spines and one to three much stouter and longer blackish central spines. Neolloydias do not want to be kept too moist even in the growing season.

### OTHER GENERA

Ancistrocactus, Cochemiea, Bartschella, Echinomastus, Escobaria, Mamillopsis, Neobesseya, Pelecyphora, Porfiria, and Solisia are other small genera referred to the pincushion cacti, although some authors, known as lumpers, have now reduced a few of these names into synonymy under the two older genera, Mammillaria and Coryphantha. Most of these are a little difficult to grow, and so should be grafted on a stout stock.

*Mamillopsis senilis,* for instance, is a beautiful small plant entirely covered with dense white spines, which prefers full sun and very porous soil and moderate amount of water in the summer season. Give it a little more water in winter and the plant will rot in a hurry.

The Neobesseyas are hardiest of the lot and can be grown outdoors in almost any part of the United States provided they receive perfect drainage, especially in winter and spring. *Neobesseya similis* and *N. missouriensis* form nice clumps, which eventually fit a bucket. When grown outdoors the plants have a tendency to draw themselves into the ground for the winter but plump up the first thing in early spring. The flowers are quite large and of a peculiar pinkish-yellow hue followed by bright red globose fruits.

## NIGHT-BLOOMING CEREUS

Night-blooming Cereus! How often have you heard this expression and how often has it been misapplied! Many people do not know that there are a great number of nocturnal cacti, and if they possess such a

plant they are under the impression that theirs is the night-blooming
Cereus. Often a plant is called "night-blooming Cereus" when in reality
it is wholly unrelated to it, as, for instance, the well known broad-leaf
cactus, Epiphyllum. We must remember that the Cerei possess certain
peculiarities that distinguish them from other cacti. In other words, every
Cereus is a Cactus but not every Cactus is a Cereus.

In the great Cactus family there are more than fifty genera belonging
to the subtribes Cereanae and Hylocereanae. Since the binomial system
was established by Linnaeus in the eighteenth century, all of these have
been included under the genus Cereus at one time or another. Many
members of these two subtribes are day-blooming, but there is also a big
group whose flowers do not open until dusk. The following is a list, al-
phabetically arranged, of mostly Britton and Rose genera of nocturnal
cacti. The names represent those accepted by most modern cactologists,
although slight differences of opinion do exist regarding a few of them,
as is to be expected.

| | | |
|---|---|---|
| Acanthocereus | Facheiroa | Peniocereus |
| Arthrocereus | Harrisia | Pilocereus |
| Binghamia | Hylocereus | Selenicereus |
| Browningia | Lemaireocereus | Stetsonia |
| Carnegiea | Leocereus | Strophocactus |
| Cephalocereus | Lophocereus | Trichocereus |
| Cereus | Mediocactus | Weberocereus |
| Dendrocereus | Monvillea | Werckleocereus |
| Eriocereus | Neoevansia | Wilmattea |
| Eulychnia | Nyctocereus | Zehntnerella |

Any of the above could be called "night-blooming Cereus," but to be
technically correct the name is applicable only to the genus Cereus as it
is understood today. However, the term is most frequently and popularly
applied to certain species in the genera Hylocereus and Selenicereus, vine-
like cacti producing the largest blooms in the Cactus family, and to the
odd turnip-rooted Peniocereus. In my opinion, it would be prudent to
confine this name to Hylocerei and Selenicerei, and the great majority of
cactus-minded folks exercise this same thought.

The name Cereus is from the Greek, signifying a torch, and refers to the candelabra-like branching of the first species known. Cereus is perhaps the oldest name given to any cactus, for it was mentioned in literature as far back as the sixteenth century. It is not definitely known who first used the name. Philip Miller, the author of the famous *Gardener's Dictionary* published in the early eighteenth century, credits the genus to P. Hermann in 1698, but the name itself was in use for more than seventy years prior to that date.

The discovery of the cacti must have left an indelible mark in the minds of the first American explorers, who referred to them as torches or candelabra and thereby aided in giving the descriptive name, Cereus, to these curious plants. Miller, however, states that the plants were not called Cereus from their resemblance to a torch alone, but also from the fact that servants burned them as torches or tapers and carried them at nights before their masters. To make the torches, the spiny specimens were cut down, dried on the ground, and dipped in oil.

The earliest illustration of a Cereus is believed to be in Oviedo's *La Historia General de las Indias,* published in 1535. This work of Oviedo is the first natural history of America, one of the rarest and most important books on the New World. Oviedo gives a general view of Spain's new American empire and the policy which should be adopted toward its people by the monarchy. The book was partially suppressed in Spain because this Spanish historian dared to tell how the Indians were abused, and this apparently accounts for the book's signal rarity. The illustration is a curious and crude woodcut which does not lend itself to critical discussion but, because of its historical value, is quite fascinating.

The first colored figure of a Cereus presumably appeared in a modest little Aztec herbal in 1552, which happens to be America's earliest treatise on Mexican medicinal plants and native remedies. The exciting and unique manuscript was written in his native tongue by an Aztec physician, Martinus de la Cruz, and was translated into Latin by a compatriot, Juannes Badianus. For more than three hundred years it lay hidden on the shelves of the Vatican Library until Dr. Charles U. Clark brought it to light in 1929. The unidentified Cereus is there called *teonochtli,* which means "Divine Cactus," and the paragraph beneath the illustration is devoted to toothache and how it can be cured with the root of this plant.

Like Oviedo's earlier woodcut, the plant in the Badianus illustration de-
fies critical naming beyond the fact that it appears to be a Cereus of
some sort, perhaps related to Lemaireocereus.

Another interesting early illustration of a night-blooming Cereus (without the flowers of course) was published in 1576 by Lobelius in his *Stirpium Adversaria Nova*. The identical figure was reproduced fifteen years
later in his *Icones Stirpium* and is now identified as *Cereus peruvianus*.
The famous herbalist, Tabernaemontanus, made use of Lobelius' figure in
his elaborate herb book on which he worked for thirty-six years before it
was published in 1588-91. However, he apparently made a new woodcut,
as the figure is slightly altered and reversed, although the revisions are
noticeable only on close scrutiny. Many of the old herbals contain repro-
ductions of the illustrations by Dodoens, Bock, Clusius, and Lobelius.
Tabernaemontanus, for one, borrowed his cuts as did many others.

In 1716 Richard Bradley published one of the first excellent figures of
a nocturnal Cereus in flower in his *History of Succulent Plants*. In a note
to the reader he stated "whatsoever figures I shall publish, will be (as
near as I can make them) perfect copies of those plants they are to represent and shall be engraved by the best hands." The figure, executed by
H. Hulsbergh, who made many other plates for Bradley, shows expert
workmanship and depicts a plant then known as *Cereus erectus maximus
americanus,* etc., or as we know it today, *Cereus peruvianus.*

Worthy of mention here are two beautiful colored plates of *Selenicereus
grandiflorus* executed by John Jacob Haid for Ehret's *Plantae Selectae,*
edited by bibliographer Christopher Trew in 1754. They show, in practically exact color and natural size, figures of stem, flower, and fruit with
their minute characteristics. There may be earlier color illustrations of a
blooming nocturnal Cereus of which I am not aware, but it is doubtful
if they can approach the beauty and exactness of Trew's publication. In
1760 Philip Miller published in his famous *Icones* another excellent color
plate of *Selenicereus grandiflorus* under the descriptive name *Cereus
scandens minor polygonus articulatus,* which he translates as "the lesser
creeping jointed Torch-thistle with many angles," but it does not com-
pare with the one in Trew's volume. Although the *Icones* was printed
in 1760, the plates were executed earlier, that of the particular Cereus on
May 25, 1756, along with five others.

## PENIOCEREUS

*Peniocereus Greggii,* native to Arizona, Texas, and New Mexico, is the only native nocturnal cactus in the United States to which the name "night-blooming Cereus" is often applied. Its stems are few and unattractive—mere "dead-looking" branches of dull gray-green protruding inconspicuously or interlaced among desert bushes. It is a difficult cactus to find when not in flower, for its top growth hides in the shelter of creosote bushes or climbs into the sturdy branches of mesquite seeking protection from devastating winds and scorching sun. These stems are leafless, lifeless in color, and possess no particular beauty of form. The most surprising thing about the plant is the root, which is a fleshy tuber resembling an overgrown turnip or carrot and weighing anywhere from five to thirty pounds—a root weighing 125 pounds has been reported. In 1949 my partner and I picked up a tuber which weighed eighty-five pounds when we were plant hunting in Arizona. These massive tubers are underground water reservoirs, but the contents are so bitter that the plant is practically immune to attack by desert rodents. The Peniocereus produces one of the fairest flowers of the desert. The tiny, hairy buds begin to swell and open in June. The large petals unfold shortly after dark and spread out into lovely waxen blossoms as big as a saucer. They wither on the morning of the following day. While they are in full bloom they fill the air with a most exquisite perfume which can be detected for some distance and betrays the location of this elusive plant. The flowers are white with a lavender tint and measure four or five inches across.

*Peniocereus Fosterianus* is a sparingly bushy Mexican plant, which was discovered in the state of Guerrero by Mulford Foster in rather dense short growth of small shrubs where it likes to grow for its support. I described and named it in 1946 for its discoverer. It is a most peculiar Peniocereus with terete stems of pencil thickness, attaining a height of seven feet, and producing white nocturnal blossoms, about five inches long.

*Peniocereus Macdougallii,* another new species which I described, is from my Mexican expedition of 1947 and was found growing in a gorge near the summit of Cerro Arenal in Oaxaca. At best, it is a scraggly shrub up to ten feet high with medium-sized, greenish-white, night-blooming flowers. Unlike the other Peniocerei, this one possesses triangular stems and has the longest spines, measuring up to three-quarters of an inch long.

### HYLOCEREUS

The genus Hylocereus is composed of about eighteen species of climbing cacti, the stems adhering to walls, tree trunks, or other supports by means of numerous aerial roots.

*Hylocereus undatus* is the best known of all night-blooming Cerei because it is widely cultivated in tropical regions. Its stem is elongated, three-angled or winged, with horny margins, and almost inconspicuous spines in its areoles. The flowers are quite succulent, especially the foliaceous scales that cover the ovary and flower tube. They attain a length of eleven to twelve inches, oblanceolate with apiculate tips, and curve just enough to form a cup of pure white which reposes in a saucer of yellowish-green sepals. The cup is filled with a great number of threadlike, cream-colored stamens arranged in two series, each thread topped by a yellowish anther. By actual count, as many as 830 stamens are produced in a single flower. A rather stout, thick, cream-colored, cylindric style protrudes from this mass of stamens and bears at its apical portion a radiating crown of yellowish stigma lobes, up to twenty-seven in number. The foliaceous scales on the ovary and floral tube are bright green, often with reddish tips and margins. The mature fruit is of a dull red color, nearly smooth, and contains white edible pulp sprinkled with blackish seed. Our specimen in the Cactus House creeps upon a trellis twenty-five feet high and then hangs suspended from one of the angle irons at the roof. The blooming season begins in early July and continues until the end of October. During the summer the whole trellis is aglow with blossoms, sometimes as many as a hundred appearing in a single night. In the fall, should the mornings be cool and cloudy, they remain open until noon.

*Hylocereus costaricensis* from Costa Rica grows well and flowers frequently in cultivation. It is a vigorous vine, perhaps the stoutest of the

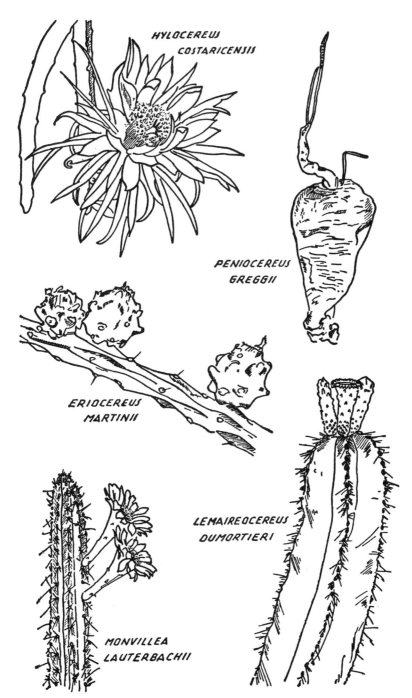

HYLOCEREUS
COSTARICENSIS

PENIOCEREUS
GREGGII

ERIOCEREUS
MARTINII

LEMAIREOCEREUS
DUMORTIERI

MONVILLEA
LAUTERBACHII

35

genus, and for this reason produces good stock for grafting purposes. The stems are more turgid than those of the preceding species and are of a bluish-white color. The young flower buds are globular, tinged a dull crimson or purple, and quite conspicuous along the more-or-less wavy margins of the joints. When fully opened, individual blossoms measure nine inches across. Scales on the ovary are closely set, greenish with deep-purple margins and tips. Toward the top of the floral tube they become more elongated and deeper green with more reddish-purple tips and margins until they merge with the narrow yellowish-green sepals. The petals are three times as broad as the sepals and are pure white. The stamens are numerous, about three and a half inches long, with creamy-white filaments and yellowish anthers. The style is a thickened, ivory-white organ, nearly nine and a half inches long, with twenty-four to twenty-seven creamy-yellow stigma lobes. In our collection, *Hylocereus costaricensis* is a very worthwhile plant. The flowers bloom throughout the summer and fall, and, since they stay open long after dawn, they can be photographed in all their beauty in daylight.

*Hylocereus Lemairei,* in my estimation, is the most beautiful species. The flowers are somewhat small, averaging only ten inches long, but possess delicate tints. Scales on the ovary and lower part of the floral tube are ovate to ovate-elongate, light green, with margins and tips blackish red-purple. Farther up the tube they become much elongated and greenish-yellow with the usual red-purple margins. The outermost sepals or uppermost throat scales are green on the outside, wax-yellow on the inside with a purplish tip. The sepals proper are wax-yellow tinged with rose color at the base. The petals are broader than the sepals, mostly oblanceolate, their lower portion pinkish, the upper white or slightly tinged yellow. Stamens, as in all Hylocerei, are very numerous; the filaments are cream and the anthers, yellow. The style is thick, sulphur-yellow, topped by a radiating cluster of twenty-nine amber-yellow stigma lobes, many of them two-cleft, a character rarely found in the cactus family.

The above three species are perhaps the most widely known and cultivated of the genus, although there are many others equally as stunning in their floral raiment. We have other species growing in the Cactus House which have not flowered as yet. It may be of interest to the reader to learn that at least two of the Hylocerei produce red flowers, *Hylocereus extensus* and *H. stenopterus*, but they are rather rare in collections.

In their native tropic haunts, plants of the genus Selenicereus either climb up the trunks of large trees by means of aerial roots or, where there are no trees and shrubs, merely trail along the ground or hang suspended from rocks and cliffs. The flowers resemble those of the Hylocereus but perhaps are not quite as succulent, nor do they possess such large conspicuous foliaceous scales on tube and ovary. Another distinguishing character is the long hair that grows out of the axils of the small scales on the ovary and perianth tube, along with bristles and felt. The stems are more slender than in the Hylocerei and mostly cylindrical and ribbed; the areoles are usually slightly elevated on small knobs and sometimes bear minute spines. The large, reddish fruit is covered with clusters of spines, bristles, and hairs. All Selenicerei are highly prized ornamentals and great favorites with amateur gardeners. The plants grow easily and rapidly in a tub provided with a trellis, where the stems soon become a tangled mass if not properly tied to the support. A juice extracted from the stems of *Selenicereus grandiflorus*, *S. coniflorus*, and allied species is prepared as a heart tonic and generally used by homeopathists. In St. Louis one pharmaceutical firm has been manufacturing "Cactina Pillets" for over fifty years, while another concern has been making "Cactegus," both products containing alkaloids from the stems of the Mexican Selenicereus.

*Selenicereus grandiflorus*, a West Indian endemic with flowers seven inches or more long, is the oldest known species. Linnaeus first described it in 1753 as a Cactus; Miller in 1768 as a Cereus; and Britton and Rose in 1909 as Selenicereus.

*Selenicereus pteranthus*, on the other hand, is the commonest species in present-day collections. Its stem is snake-like, bluish-green often tinged with purple, strongly four-angled, bearing in its areoles small conical black spines. The flowers appear in June and complete their blooming cycle within one month. It might be added that they are highly susceptible to daylight, and they close with the approach of dawn even on days that tend to be cool or cloudy; at least, this has been the case at the Missouri Botanical Garden since 1931. The blooms of *Selenicereus pteranthus* average eleven inches long. The outer perianth segments or sepals are linear, about three and a half inches long, yellowish with reddish tints, while the outermost are dull bronze colored to purplish-brown; inner perianth segments or petals are pure white, spatulate-oblong with acuminate tips. Stamens are very numerous, greenish to cream colored, the upper row upturned slightly at the tips where the anthers appear, shorter than the unequal, elongated lower stamens which recline on the side of the tube and are attached along its inner face two and three-quarters inches. The style is cream-colored, light green at the base, nine and a half inches long, and supports about fifteen linear, yellowish-green stigma lobes at the apex. Long, white, silky hairs and bristles are borne in the axils of the tiny red-tipped greenish scales that cover the ovary and the furrowed floral tube.

Of the other Selenicerei, some flowers are larger than others and the outer floral envelopes may have varying shades of yellow, green, or purple, while the hairy ornament may also differ in color. Generally, the species are practically identical but may be distinguished by the vegetative characters and areole armament. At least twenty species are recognized by most authorities. The Garden's collection of Selenicerei is not too exhaustive, although a representative lot is being grown, including *Selenicereus coniflorus, S. grandiflorus, S. hondurensis, S. pteranthus, S. Donkelaari, S. Boeckmannii, S. Macdonaldiae, S. vagans,* and several others whose identity is still shrouded in doubt.

## ACANTHOCEREUS

An Acanthocereus plant is to be found in practically every cactus collection. The plants are usually weak, elongated, and have many joints, while their funnel-shaped, night-blooming white flowers are usually large and rather beautiful. Young growth is often terete, ribbed, and soft-spiny, while mature stems are often strongly three-angled and stiff-spined. New growth is so puzzling that many people ask whether the plants are grafted.

*Acanthocereus pentagonus,* which was described meagerly by Linnaeus in 1753, is one of the oldest known species. Stems at first are erect, but being weak, soon make arches and root wherever they strike the ground. Permitted to grow like this outdoors in warm climates, the plant will form large colonies or thickets in a short time. Young growth has six to eight low ribs, and the ridges produce areoles with numerous short acicular spines. Adult growth is three- to five-angled with conical to subulate spiny armament. Several races are reported, and some authorities separate them into two or three distinct species.

*Acanthocereus pentagonus* is commonly called "Barbed-wire Cactus." Its flowers are about seven inches long, the floral tube and ovary greenish-blue bearing a few conspicuous areoles with tannish felt and several small varicolored spines. Sepals are light green; petals white, narrow, one-quarter inch wide. Stamens are very numerous, the filaments white, the anthers pale yellow. Style is six and a quarter inches long, creamish, topped by twelve similarly colored stigma lobes. This and *Acanthocereus floridanus* are the only Acanthocerei that are found wild in the United States.

*Acanthocereus occidentalis,* from the western coast of Mexico, is another fascinating species. It bears flowers nearly nine inches long, the tube and very small ovary taking up more than three quarters of its length. The tube expands into a wide throat and is filled with a mass of erect stamens one to two inches long, the filaments being white and the anthers, buff-yellow. From the center of this mass protrudes a thickened style, the apex divided into thirteen linear, pale-yellow, stigma lobes. The petals are ensiform, white or slightly tinged with light yellowish green toward the tips, sometimes also flushed with pink. Throat scales are lanceolate, green, up to an inch long, while the sepals are linear, acuminate, lighter in color, and nearly two inches long.

*Acanthocereus colombianus* from northern South America is still another handsome species, but, according to Dr. Leon Croizat, this name was reduced to synonymy under *Acanthocereus Pitajaya* in 1943. The flower is one of the largest in the Cactaceae, measuring up to a foot in length. The floral tube and throat are approximately nine inches long, light green on the outside, slightly ridged. Petals are white and number around forty, the innermost being somewhat shorter. Sepals are longer than the petals, brown-green to light green or flushed with pinkish-brown in the middle. Stamens, which are attached to the wall of the tube about three and a half inches above the ovary, possess white filaments and light yellow anthers. The style is slender, white, nine inches long, and bears at the top thirteen cream-colored stigma lobes. Other species are cultivated and admired for their ornamental value.

### ERIOCEREUS AND HARRISIAS

The genera Eriocereus and Harrisia are very much alike, the chief distinguishing features occurring in the fruits. The Eriocerei are usually vine-like and trailing or procumbent, with red and dehiscent (splitting) fruits. Harrisias, on the other hand, are mostly semi-erect with yellowish or orange-red fruits that are indehiscent (not splitting). The Eriocerei, of which there are about eleven common species, have their home in South America, south of the equator. Harrisia is native to Florida, the Bahamas, and the West Indies.

*Eriocereus Martinii* from Argentina is the most popular species. It is a clambering, night-flowering vine whose stems attain a length of many feet. Adult and young growth is four- to six-angled, dotted with conspicuous circular areoles from which a stout, straw-colored, black-tipped spine protrudes. Flowers average about nine inches long and are quite odoriferous. They are borne singly at areoles near the ends of the long branches. The ovaries are tuberculate and bright green, maturing into crimson-red fruits which are produced abundantly and adorn the dark green stems for many months. The sepals are lanceolate, light green, often flushed with red or pink at the tips. Petals are oblanceolate to obovate, white with a greenish base or flushed with pale green through the middle. Stamens appear in two series, the inner ones being the longest and attached to the tube all the way up to the throat, while the outer ones are attached to the mouth of the throat in a single row. Style is seven inches long, light green, topped by twelve linear, obtuse, green stigma lobes. The seeds of this species germinate very easily and the seedlings grow rapidly, producing flowers within five to seven years.

*Eriocereus tortuosus* likewise hails from Argentina. Adult stems are stout and very spiny. Flowers measure about seven or eight inches long, and have a tendency to remain open on cool, cloudy days for several hours. Ovary is tuberculate, deep grape-green with minute purple scales bearing whitish hairs in their axils. Flower tube and throat are slightly lighter in color and often purplish tinted, their topmost scales merging into sepals. The sepals are light green at the base, lighter to nearly white through the center, and usually pinkish along the margins and apex. Petals are somewhat shorter, obovate in outline, pure white or faintly greenish at base. Stamens are in two series, a single row attached at the mouth of the throat and the rest all along the lower portion of the throat down the flower tube. Style is light green with fourteen linear, chartreuse-yellow stigma lobes.

*Eriocereus Bonplandii* is a four-angled plant. Its flowers attain a size of ten inches, and the petals are larger than those of the two species just described, being at least four inches long. The inner two rows are pure white except for the base, while the outer are pale green throughout. The sepals are light green, those outermost often tinged slightly purple-brown at the tips. Stamens in two series, the lowermost attached to within a half inch of the ovary. Style is light green with sixteen light-yellow stigma lobes.

Most of the Harrisias are upright-growing cacti and ideal for the greenhouse, producing blossoms in abundance. Three species, *Harrisia fragrans, H. aboriginum,* and *H. Simpsonii,* grow wild in Florida; *Harrisia Earlei, H. eriophora, H. Fernowii* and *H. Taylori,* in Cuba; and the rest in Jamaica, Puerto Rico, and the Bahamas.

### MONVILLEA

*Monvillea Cavendishii* is one of the most prolific nocturnal bloomers of the slender, clambering or semi-erect types. Flowers make their appearance in early April and continue to bloom way into September. The plant is more or less branched with stems which are cylindrical and quite spiny. The flowers are white, up to five and a half inches long, borne toward the tops of last year's growths. The sepals have a reddish or greenish hue, and the petals are pure white. Stamens have white filaments and creamy-tan anthers. The white style, a trifle longer than the stamens, has twelve to fourteen white stigma lobes. The fruit is a glabrous, spineless, reddish "apple" about two inches long, which contains edible white pulp sprinkled with a great number of shining black seeds. This one is the most popular and best known of the group.

*Monvillea Lauterbachii* is a delightful partner, possessing medium-sized flowers which are quite dazzling. Sepals are greenish with lighter margins while the petals are entirely white. The slender whitish-green style with its sixteen linear, white, stigma lobes protrudes from a circular mass of stamens.

### OTHER GENERA

Nyctocereus is a slender-stemmed, many ribbed, spiny genus of ornamental cacti growing wild in Mexico, Guatemala, and Nicaragua. *Nyctocereus serpentinus,* which first came into prominence at the beginning of the nineteenth century, is the best known of the group. Many know it as the "Snake Cactus" or "Serpent Cactus" on account of its stems which clamber through bushes, over walls, or creep and hang in snake-like fashion. Flowers of this night-blooming Cereus are white and attain a size of seven and a half inches. Its stems serve as excellent grafting stocks.

Mediocactus is a South American genus containing two species of epiphytes, but only one, *Mediocactus coccineus,* is in cultivation. In vegetative character it looks much like a Hylocereus, but the flowers are shaped more like those of a Selenicereus without the hairs on tube and ovary. The flower is large, funnel-shaped, somewhat fragrant, at least ten and a half inches long; sepals linear, bright green, widely spreading; petals semi-erect, oblong to obovate with serrate apices, white; stamens numerous, creamy-yellow with identically colored exserted style bearing at its top fifteen linear, light-greenish, stigma lobes.

Weberocereus is a genus of Central American cacti with stems resembling a slender Hylocereus, or, better still, a form of Rhipsalis. Only three species are known, and these possess rather insignificant blossoms of light pink, rose color, or white.

Werckleocereus is another Central American genus of epiphytic habit, much resembling a Hylocereus. However, it may be distinguished by its medium-sized, short, funnel-form flowers which bear many blackish-spined and black-felty areoles on ovary and flower tube. Unfortunately, both of these last two genera are rarely found in collections in this country.

*Wilmattea minutiflora* grows in Guatemala and Honduras. Its slender stems resemble those of Hylocereus, but its flowers are much smaller with a narrow limb and with a very short tube. There is only one species.

*Strophocactus Wittii* is a rare Brazilian endemic which inhabits swampy forests of the Amazon region. Its flat, Epiphyllum-like stems twist about the trunks of trees and produce elongated, large flowers that resemble those of Selenicereus. At present it is not known in cultivation anywhere, but it is a novelty which should be reintroduced.

Of the stout, columnar, nocturnal Cerei, the Lophocereus is an interesting genus native to Mexico and southern Arizona. The generic name, signifying crested Cereus, refers to the bristly top of the flowering stem which is columnar and quite stout. Because of the long bristles on the fertile joints it is sometimes given the name "Whisker Cactus." The most sought-after species is a monstrous form commonly known as the "Totem Pole Cactus." Its flowers are rather small, about one and a half inches long, opening early in the evening and closing the following morning.

The genus Trichocereus contains many types of growth habit. Quite a few of the species grow as low bushes; some are prostrate and form dense thickets; while a few assume gigantic proportions. The stems are usually characterized by many ribs, thickly set with areoles and usually very spiny. The large, nocturnal, funnel-shaped flowers are mostly white, often highly fragrant. About twenty-eight species are recorded from the Andes Mountains of South America. Some of the species, as *Trichocereus Spachianus,* are used as stock in grafting, but with us they have a tendency to rot if not carefully watched.

The genus Lemaireocereus boasts very tall cacti. Most of them branch from the base or from low trunks, the branches growing erect in closely set fashion remindful of the pipes of an organ. Most of the species bear flowers that open during the day, but there are a few like *Lemaireocereus hystrix, L. quevedonis, L. Standleyi,* and *L. Cartwrightianus* with nocturnal blossoms. More than twenty species of Lemaireocereus are listed, each one highly ornamental. Their range of distribution extends from southern Arizona through Mexico to Peru and Venezuela and into Cuba. The stems of all are unexcelled as stock for grafting the globular kinds of cacti.

Eulychnia is a Chilean genus of four species inhabiting dry hills. In some parts of the Chilean deserts these form the dominant feature, but as yet they are not plentiful in American collections. The white or pinkish flowers are both diurnal and nocturnal.

Facheiroa is a rare Brazilian and Peruvian genus of bushy habit not well known in collections as yet. It is much branched and very spiny, its nocturnal flowers borne on a cephalium or head consisting of a compact mass of reddish-brown wool or hair. The flowers are very small and white.

Zehntnerella is a tall, slender, much-branching genus from Brazil. One species, *Zehntnerella squamulosa,* is known to exist, and it is rarely seen in collections. It is said to produce very small white nocturnal flowers with many long hairs inside the throat.

Binghamia is a bushy, more or less branched cactus with the habit of Trichocereus, but lower and with smaller, white, nocturnal flowers. The genus is confined to Peru. The few species are of slow growth and very shy bloomers.

Browningia is one of the most grotesque genera in the Cactaceae. It contains a lone species, *Browningia candelaris,* which grows at high altitudes in Chile and Peru. Specimens produce a single upright trunk with curiously spreading or drooping branches at the top. The funnel-shaped flowers are a little curved, nearly white, and open in the evening.

Cephalocereus and Pilocereus are two closely allied genera with members native to Florida, Mexico, West Indies, Guatemala, Colombia, Venezuela, Peru, Brazil, and Ecuador. For the most part, they are tall, erect, and columnar, with small bell-shaped flowers. The most outstanding species is *Cephalocereus senilis,* the famous Old Man Cactus of Mexico which every cactus fancier desires to possess.

Stetsonia is a monotypic genus of Argentina with large nocturnal flowers produced on the upper part of the branches. The tree attains immense proportions and is much branched. It is an extremely slow grower but small plants are plentiful and available in the trade.

Arthrocereus and Leocereus are rather rare Brazilian genera infrequently, if at all, seen in collections; however, the first is being propagated in California.

Dendrocereus is a Cuban genus, its one species, *Dendrocereus nudiflorus*, being a thick-trunked, many-branched tree with large white flowers. Our original specimen was damaged severely during the hailstorm of May, 1927, but it flowered and fruited before it died a few years later and seedlings from it have become established. The plant is still rare in collections.

The stately but thorny Carnegiea, called Saguaro in the Southwest, is one of the largest and noblest of all cacti. It towers majestically, with raised, candelabra-like arms, above all other desert vegetation. Only one species, *Carnegiea gigantea,* exists and it is plentiful in Arizona which state has adopted its flower officially. The trunk and branches of the Saguaro are fluted and armed with stout spines set in long straight rows. In late spring white waxy blossoms adorn the tips of the stems, growing singly but close together and giving a beautiful clustered effect.

The genus Cereus contains nearly thirty species most of which are upright, tall, and much branched. The best flowering species in our collection is *Cereus validus*. Its slender branches reach the roof of the Cactus House and produce several hundred blossoms during the summer season. The fruits, which are produced copiously, have a habit of splitting while still attached to the branches, revealing the rich crimson pulp within. Visitors who are not acquainted with cactus flowers often refer to the colorful dehiscing fruits as flowers.

The night-blooming Cerei, on the whole, are easy to manage and one or two forms should be included even in the humblest of collections. Watching the lovely blossoms unfurl their immaculate petals is a thrill of a lifetime and you will invite your friends to enjoy this rare spectacle with you. A cactus fan thinks that such dazzling beauty and fragrance can be found in no other plant.

## JUNGLE CACTI

The average person thinks of cacti only as despicable plants growing in the hottest and driest.regions of the desert. It is wrong to believe that all cacti inhabit hot, arid lands and that all are wickedly armed and ugly to look at. What a great surprise is in store for you if you are one of the doubting Thomases!

In the moist warm jungles of tropical and subtropical America is a group of plants that enjoy the same kind of life as ferns, bromels, orchids, begonias, and aroids. Perched high above the ground in crotches and on the branches and trunks of trees, epiphytic cacti are not subject to climatic caprices as are the desert kinds. The plants, snugly anchored to the rough bark by roots, escape the direct rays of the sun as well as rough winds that blow unabated in more open spaces. The leafy canopy of trees allows filtered light to reach the plants; it diminishes the force of a tropical rainstorm and permits a gentle spraying rather than a rough beating. It also permits free circulation of air, and the humid warmth that ascends from the dank floor is beneficial.

The true species of epiphytic cacti are essentially plants with long or short flattened branches with notches along the margins, in which the areoles are located. If they are not flattened, they assume cylindrical or angular stems branching and rebranching until a heavy pendent mass is the result. Some of these branches may reach a length of twenty feet. Many of the Rhipsalis, for instance, hang in an extremely graceful manner from the giant branches of forest trees and therefore make excellent basket plants in our greenhouses and sun porches.

The true Epiphyllums are mostly of night-blooming habit with flowers described as lily-like and funnel-shaped, up to nearly a foot in length. These are the species that have been crossed with colorful day-blooming kinds which produced the flamboyant hybrids, now popularly called "orchid cacti" by many growers because their flowers rival and even excel the orchid in color. Commercial growers have, since about 1935, advertised the Epiphyllum hybrids under orchid cacti, feeling that the name holds a more popular appeal than the botanical name. However, the Epiphyllum Society of America, whose members are dedicated to a better understanding of those plants, is trying to discourage its usage, because some of the public is a little confused about the term and many of them are under the erroneous impression that these hybrids are orchids rather than true cacti. I'm sure the general public will persist in using the name for a long time!

For better acquaintance with jungle cacti and for an understanding of their culture, I will attempt to name and describe all of the diverse forms under this grouping. There are two chief subtribes to be dealt with: the Epiphyllanae and the Rhipsalidanae. The former contains species with unusually large flowers, whereas the latter normally exhibit very small flowers but in greater abundance.

Usually, all the jungle cacti inhabit forest trees, fallen logs, or moist rock faces in the rain forests of South America, the hot steaming lands of Central America and the West Indies, as well as the dense wooded tracts of Mexico. They prefer an aerial life, anchoring their roots in the fissured bark of trees or depositing them in crotches and pockets where humus is stored. Not only are they found on trees, but some even find security in cracks and crevices of stony escarpments or in the cushions of moss draping moist barranca walls.

We call these inhabitants "epiphytes" because they attach themselves to other objects for security only. Their nourishment comes from the air or from the humus in which they grow—never from their hosts. If the latter were true they would have to be called parasites, like the Mistletoe which actually steals nutrients from its host and often causes the death of its benefactor. None of the cacti are said to be parasitic.

Epiphytic cacti seem to prefer the company of other plants in the wild. On my exploration trips I noticed huge masses of lichens and mosses as well as familiar flowering plants, such as the orchids, begonias, peperomias, and lush aroids. From this environment we get our ideas how best to treat the plants in our homes and how to duplicate those requirements. First of all, jungle cacti will require a fairly loose porous soil, semiacid in character, that can be perfectly drained after each drenching. Since the plants prefer an aerial position, it gives us an idea that they desire a location allowing adequate circulation of air and alternate light and shade.

The amount of space at your disposal will determine the number and varieties that can be grown. The average window sill will not accommodate many of the large flowered types like the Epiphyllums, but a few pots of Zygocactus, Schlumbergera, and Rhipsalis are possible. Epiphyllums and their hybrids are more suitable for small greenhouses, sun porches, and spacious bay windows. Showcases in stores are not to be overlooked, either.

The Epiphyllums and their gorgeous hybrids, the Orchid Cacti, will be dealt with first. The true species, as already stated, possess mostly white flowers which open in the black of night. Their growth is erect at first but later tends to become pendant or hanging. Since they need lots of space, they are fit subjects for the greenhouse or porch. The flowers are very large and showy, with a tube which is often long and slender. Sometimes there is a peculiar bending just above the ovary likened to a saxophone or Dutchman's pipe. The flowers last only for one night and usually become limp and drooping at the crack of dawn. There are around sixteen true species, not all of them in cultivation, however. Probably the best known and most cultivated is *Epiphyllum oxypetalum*.

*Epiphyllum oxypetalum* is found in all parts of Central America and extends to some of the South American countries on the south and into Mexico in the north. The dense growth becomes woody at base from which long, thin, often wavy branches arise. The branches possess a recurving habit so that the tips often reach the ground and root, thus having a tendency to creep. These branches may attain a length of nine feet or more. The species is universally cultivated in all parts of the world, and in the Midwest growers often refer to it as "Night-blooming Cereus," although this is a misnomer as the plant does not belong to the Cereus tribe at all. Whenever this cactus flowers in the St. Louis area you can be sure that people will call the local newspapers to announce the event. The flowers are long and stout with a reddish tube having a few narrow scales. They are quite fragrant especially when several are in bloom at the same time. The flowers average about twelve inches in length including the tube which is at least six inches long. Ordinarily the flower tube is red tinted topped by reddish to amber sepals and oblong white petals; but as it is a variable species, there is also a form with a greenish tube and greenish-white sepals.

My good friend, Tom MacDougall, who has collected a number of wild forms of Epiphyllums in Mexico, states that *Epiphyllum oxypetalum* was common along the trail between the Coatzacoalcos and Chalchijapa rivers in Oaxaca. There it grew with another species, *Epiphyllum pumilum,* which originally was thought to be a Guatemalan endemic. Although he noticed some of the plants on trees, many more were growing in shallow humus on isolated masses of limestone that projected well above the forest floor. Both of these species are cultivated at the Missouri Botanical Garden from stock brought up from Mexico.

*Epiphyllum pumilum* can hardly be called a robust grower. It is instead a rather graceful plant with unusually small flowers—only three inches long. These are quite fragrant, unfurling at night and remaining open late in the morning—until noon on a cool day. At the Garden, blossoms make their appearance in July. There are only a few perianth segments (sepals and petals), approximately seventeen in number, the outer ones much narrower and greenish white, the inner white and at least an inch broad. Although the growth at first is erect, later it becomes quite pendant and therefore is recommended for basket culture. This is one Epiphyllum that is small enough to be included in a window collection.

*Epiphyllum Pittieri,* native to Costa Rica, which sometimes is mistaken for the preceding, is another rather small flowered species. The Costa Rican plant seems to be bushier with heavier, slightly larger blossoms possessing more perianth segments and a pinkish style which is deeper colored toward the base. The style of *Epiphyllum pumilum* is white throughout. It is an abundant bloomer, flowering several times during the year. Although advertised as the baby of all Epiphyllums, I think this title rightly belongs to *Epiphyllum pumilum* which perhaps is not as well known a species as *Epiphyllum Pittieri.*

*Epiphyllum phyllanthus* appears to be the oldest species on record, as it was known as early as 1753. This species enjoys a wide distributional range which extends from Panama down to Peru and Brazil. It is a much-branched, flat-leaved cactus with rather long, white, nocturnal flowers. The odd thing about the flower is the extremely long tube of pencil thickness, twelve to thirteen inches long, and a comparatively small corolla with petals only an inch long. The long, slender, reddish style bears short white stigma lobes. The fruits are extremely colorful, being oblong, slightly furrowed, vivid red, and three inches or more long.

*Epiphyllum Hookeri* is another old-fashioned species which at first was erroneously mistaken for *Epiphyllum phyllanthus* because it also has a long, slender flower tube. It comes from Venezuela, where it grows in large masses on the rocks and trees. The flowers are scentless, with pure white petals and narrow, greenish-pink sepals. The style is rather colorful, being yellow at base, carmine in the middle, and pinkish at the top with ten to twelve radiating, yellow, stigma lobes.

*Epiphyllum guatemalense* is a giant-flowered, narrow-petaled species which is very easy to grow. As its specific name suggests, it was first found in Guatemala about forty-one years ago, but it also grows wild in Chiapas, Mexico, where Tom MacDougall observed it growing on large trees in company with the beautiful orchid, *Cattleya Skinneri.* Not only did he find it in great abundance on the road between Tapachula and Cacahoatan, but in several other districts toward Oaxaca. I find it a vigorous grower, its coarsely crenate, flat, green branches supporting night-blooming blossoms, nine inches or more in diameter. The flower petals are very narrow, and sepals are scale-like. The long, glossy style supports orange stigma lobes.

*Epiphyllum strictum* is a popular and common species found in most collections. It is a sturdy, erect plant with woody base and rather stout branches nearly two inches broad. It is a good bloomer, the flowers appearing from July through October. They are moderately large with narrow, pointed, white petals. The pink to cerise style with yellow stigma lobes is quite prominent. This plant is common in Mexico and Guatemala and is found as far south as Panama.

*Epiphyllum crenatum* has been used extensively in hybridizing. It is notable for the fact that the flowers are diurnal and stay open for several days. Most of the other true species bloom at night. It is a sturdy and robust plant with woody terete stems and rather stiff, deeply cut, glaucous branches that exhibit a thick midrib. The large flowers are cream colored to greenish-yellow, delicately scented. It hails from Honduras and Guatemala.

*Epiphyllum stenopetalum* from Mexico is somewhat similar to *Epiphyllum strictum* but possesses wider, flexible joints, and its flowers have many narrow petals and a somewhat unpleasant odor. It is a robust grower and can be used as a basket specimen, as can most of the Epiphyllums.

*Epiphyllum macropterum* hails from Costa Rica and is distinguished by horny-angled branches and very large flowers that are day-blooming and fragrant. The flower also displays a curved tube which is characteristic of the better known *Epiphyllum oxypetalum.*

*Epiphyllum anguliger* and *E. Darrahii* are two outstanding Mexican species. Both bear flowers that are neither large nor especially showy, but the pattern of the stems is so unique that it makes these two species attractive at all times. The branches are deeply notched almost to the thickened midrib and somewhat resemble the backbone of a fish, so that Fishbone Cactus is an appropriate name for them. Although the growth is variable, *Epiphyllum Darrahii* possesses ascending and more pointed stem lobes than *Epiphyllum anguliger.* The stem lobes of the latter are more rounded at the tips. The flowers, practically identical, have some distinguishing differences. *Epiphyllum Darrahii* has a long, slender, green tube with very few greenish appressed scales and about twelve lemon-yellow sepals, with mostly pure white but often yellow-tipped petals. On the other hand, the flowers of *Epiphyllum anguliger* are perhaps slightly smaller with no scales on the shorter flower tube and with paler green-brown sepals and faintly green tinged petals. Both species are fragrant.

*Epiphyllum lepidocarpum* is a small Costa Rican cactus with glossy green branches less than two inches wide. Flowers are quite pretty, about eight inches long, with a greenish-red tube supporting reddish scales and topped by pale carmine sepals and pure white petals.

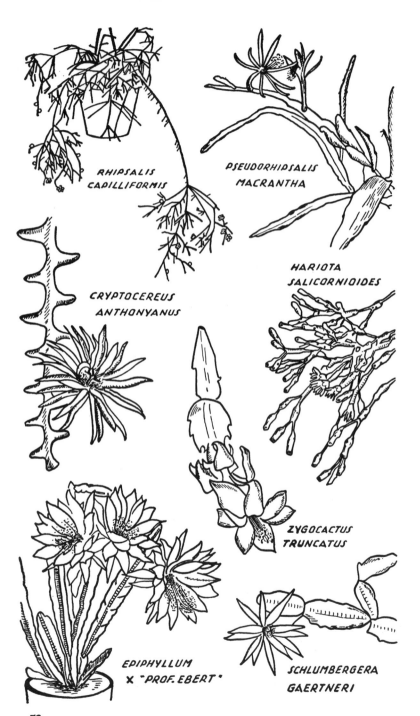

RHIPSALIS
CAPILLIFORMIS

PSEUDORHIPSALIS
MACRANTHA

CRYPTOCEREUS
ANTHONYANUS

HARIOTA
SALICORNIOIDES

ZYGOCACTUS
TRUNCATUS

EPIPHYLLUM
X "PROF. EBERT"

SCHLUMBERGERA
GAERTNERI

*Epiphyllum cartagense* is a tall, much branched, coarsely crenate plant which apparently is composed of several races exhibiting variable marginal differences in stems, size of flowers, and color of the style.

*Epiphyllum caudatum* and *E. grandilobum* are in cultivation but are not clearly defined. The former is a Mexican plant characterized by a supposedly long, acuminate or tail-like growth at the tip of the branches, while the latter has moderately long but extremely wide branches that give it its specific name. Both species are nocturnal bloomers.

### EPIPHYLLUM HYBRIDS

Although the true species of Epiphyllum possess large and fairly beautiful flowers, they are not as colorful as their hybrids which come in innumerable shapes, sizes, and floral colors. More than a century ago the first European hybridist made a successful cross between a Broadleaf Cactus and a Sun Cereus, combining the best traits of both plants. Later, others took up the work, using other related material and, by method of pollination, cross-pollination, selfing and selection, were able to produce a brilliant color range in these new hybrids. By 1897 at least 370 names were listed by Charles Simon, breeder, Saint-Ouen, Paris.

It can be safely said that at the present time there must be at least 3,000 different Orchid Cacti in existence, and new ones are being added annually to the growing list. To recount the history of Epiphyllum hybridizing it would be necessary to devote many more pages than could be allotted in this book. However, it is permissible to sketch hybridization in the United States and mention present-day breeders.

American interest in Epiphyllum breeding dates back to about 1926, when Mr. H. M. Wegener of Los Angeles began to import the European hybrids. Their fascination led him to experimentation and soon he began to produce many original hybrids of his own. Dr. R. W. Poindexter and Mrs. Clarion Steele were also listed as early importers of European hybrids and, like Mr. Wegener, began to produce many fine crosses. Dr. Poindexter, more than any other Epiphyllum fancier, was influential in popularizing these plants in this country. It was he who published a large catalog in 1941 dealing exclusively with Orchid Cacti.

Present American hybridizers are Mrs. Gertrude W. Beahm, Cactus Pete, the Coolidge Gardens, and Mrs. Theresa Monmonier, all of whose establishments except the last I was able to inspect on my trips to California.

Since it would not be possible to list and describe all the known hybrids here, I must refer you to catalogs and lists put out by the commercial firms and also to the *Bulletin of the Epiphyllum Society of America* which is conducting research that aids in the standardization of names. However, in order to aid you in choosing varieties, I will list a number of these hybrids under color categories, but it is to be remembered that many of the flowers may have more than one outstanding color in their make-up. Only those horticultural varieties are listed which are readily obtainable in the trade.

## GROUP ONE—WHITE, CREAM, YELLOW

| | | |
|---|---|---|
| Admiral Togo | Diamond Lil | Ivory Queen |
| Albino | Dove of Peace | Katy-Did |
| Albus Superbissimus | Eastern Morn | Larseni |
| Amarillo | Eden | Londonii |
| Angelino | Elfe | Los Angeles Lucite |
| Azusena | Emerald Isle | Lucite |
| Baby | Eskimo | Luna |
| Baby Doll | Estrellita | Lyra |
| Ballet Russe | Ferdinand Schmoll | Madam Chiang Kai-Shek |
| Ben's Laura | Francisco | Madonna |
| Beulah | Frau von Schiller | Magnolia |
| Blanco | Gardenia | Mammoth Moon |
| Bridal Veil | Ghost | Milky Way |
| Buttercup | Gold Star | Moonlight |
| Castnori | Gretchen Steudte | Moonlove |
| Champagne | Gretna Green | Mt. Lofty |
| Charles Larkin | Halo | Niagara |
| Citrine | Heaven Scent | Padua |
| Cooperii | Helianthus | Paper Moon |
| Crystal Cup | Iced Glory | Paul de Longpre |
| Desert Gold | Icicle | Peace |
| Deutschland | Ivory | Phantom |

Phoebe
Phosphor
Polar Bear
Pond Lily
Pres. F. D. Roosevelt
Regina del Chiaro
San Jacinto
Santa Fe
Serenidad
Seven Up

Shalimar
Shasta
Sitka
Snow Drop
Star of Bethlehem
Star Dust
Sun Glow
Theme Song
Towhead
Triumph

Westfalen
White Fairy
White Flame
White Peacock
White Lotus
White Moon
Wodan
Wrayii
Yellow Violet
Young Nun

## GROUP TWO—ORANGE TO AUTUMN SHADES

Apollo
Artista
Autumn
Aztec
Bliss
Brahma
California Beauty
Camillo Schneider
Cassandra
Cleone
Countess Estelle Doheny
Cup of Gold
Curt Backeberg
Dante
Darrell
Denis Kucera
Desert Sunrise
Dr. von Roeder
Enchantress
Eve
Fedala
Fiesta
Flamenco

Flamingo
Flor del Sol
Freidrich Boedecker
Gabriel's Horn
Gloria
Golden Emblem
Golden Gleam
Hawaii
Indian Summer
Kadolia
Lackneri
Leonotis
Lodestar
Miss Beverly
Miss Santa Monica
Navajo
Nellie Cantwell
New York
Oberst P. M. Kuhnrich
Orange Nymph
Paracutin
Pirate Gold
Pride of Ventura

Richard Diener
San Antonio
San Bernardino
Sequoia
Silver Moon
Snow Queen
Southland
Speciosa
Spider Queen
Stellette
Sun Beam
Sun Goddess
Sunrise
Susquehanna
Tangerine
Tangiers
Titian
Topaz
Topsy-Turvy
Trocadero
Tululosa
Valencia

## GROUP THREE—RED

| | | |
|---|---|---|
| Alta Scott | Emperatrice | Miss Nancy Bell |
| Amber Queen | Erebella | Mojave |
| American Girl | Erebus | Nomad |
| Amulet | Etinsolate | Otto Siepke |
| Arabian Night | Etoile de Contiche | Paula Knebel |
| Aristocrat | Fasan | Pegasus |
| Atlas | Fluff | Poinsettia |
| Bahia | Francheski | Profusion |
| Bali | Francois Verhaert | Purple Flame |
| Bambino | Friedrich Werner Beul | Red Letter |
| Bandana | Friend Wegener | Red Wing |
| Banner Red | Fruhling | Repertoire |
| Barbara Frietchie | Gamut | Riot |
| Belgian Pfau | Garnet | Rottkapchen |
| Black Monarch | Germania | Rugosa |
| Blaue Flamme | Gypsy Girl | Scott E. Haselton |
| Bleeding Heart | Heart's Desire | Senorita |
| Brilliant | Hermosus | Siegfried |
| Cabochon | Imp | Sleepy Hollow |
| Carmen | Inferno | Stern von Erlau |
| Cartwheel | Inner Glow | Tarantula |
| Cattleya | Janet | Thorinne |
| Ceka | Jenkinsonii | Thunder Bird |
| Dark Victory | Jericho | Thunder Cloud |
| Dominion | Jezebel | Tiffany |
| Dragon's Eye | Jolibois | Treasure Chest |
| Dr. Houghton | Jules Schlumberger | Tulip |
| Ebonite | Katrinka | Vive Rouge |
| Edah | Kismet | Viviana |
| El Monte | Livingston | Warrier |
| El Rey | Mikado | |

## GROUP FOUR—LIGHT TO DEEP PINKS

| | | |
|---|---|---|
| Adonis | Alice Sergeant | Bella |
| Adonita | Allurosa | Blush |
| Agatha | Argus | Blush O' Dawn |

Bohemienne
Bonnie Brae
Cantabile
Carnation
Celestine
Charm
Cinderella
Cindy
Clarabella
Dark Daphne
Dawn
Day in Spring
Delhi
Deliciosa
Deutsche Kaiserin
Duchess of Windsor
Duke of Windsor
Eleesa
Ensemble
Euphrosine
Fairy Queen
Giant Empress
Grace Marie

Harmony
Haviland
Hollydale
Kaiserin Import
Lady Edna
Lady Godiva
Lady Irene
Latonia
Lila
Lilac Time
Mauvette
Maxwellton
Mermaid
Miss Margaret Truman
Misty Isle
Mrs. Bess Truman
Nanette
Neon
Nilmah
Normandie
Orchid Beauty
Orchid Shower

Padre
Pandora
Paradise Queen
Pastello
Pink Nymph
Princess Pat
Romeo
Rosalie
Rose Blush
Rose Marie Rosetta
Rose of Monterrey
Rose Tourney
Rosea Stellata
Rosetta
Royal Robe
September Morn
Show Girl
Springtime
Starlla Lee
Sweet Briar
Tahoe
Walkure

## GROUP FIVE—PURPLE

Anton Gunther
Augusta von Szombathy
Bambi
Bewitched
Bizerte
Buenos Noches
Concord
Dr. Werdermann
Eleanora Prochaska
Elkhart
Frau H. M. Wegener

Frau Martha Siepke
Frau Stanka Stozier
Gertrude W. Beahm
Jacques Courant
Joseph de Laet
Minuet
Muriel
Orchid Supreme
Paradise
Persia
Pride of Bell

Prof. Ebert
Purple Delight
Queen Katherine
Sherman E. Beahm
Transvaal
Triumphe de Entwerd
Uncle Sam
Vesuvius
Whirlaway
Wonderland

### CHRISTMAS CACTUS

Scarcely any collector of house plants is without the old-fashioned Christmas Cactus, which has been a favorite ever since it was introduced more than a century ago. It is a bushy plant of graceful arching habit, composed of thin, glossy leaf-like joints up to two inches long. Zygomorphic flowers are extremely beautiful and possess a distinct shape from most other epiphytic cacti. The flower tube is sharply bent upward above the ovary from which petaloid scales arise that have the same color as the true petals at the end of the tube. The corolla is two-lipped as a result of the longer petals being distinctly reflexed. The unequal white stamens appear in a dense cluster against the upper side of the corolla, and the purple stigma is slightly extended beyond the anthers.

The taxonomic position of the Christmas Cactus is a puzzle; and, although several specialists have attempted to place its true identity, it is still a questionable venture. What the nurserymen usually sell as *Zygocactus truncatus* is a plant having fleshy, flattened, leaf-like joints with rounded crenations and handsome, deep rose, nearly regular flowers, but the true Zygocactus must have an irregular or zygomorphic perianth. The Christmas Cactus common in the trade is apparently more correctly a Schlumbergera, but the specific name is uncertain. My good friend, Dr. Reid V. Moran, who has delved somewhat extensively into the taxonomic problem, suggests that *Schlumbergera Bridgesii* is the correct name for the Christmas Cactus. Only time will tell whether his assumption is correct and the name universally accepted. It might be mentioned here that the genus Schlumbergera is very similar to Zygocactus except that its flowers are symmetrical with much narrower petals disposed in star-like fashion and the fruit is always angled. In Zygocactus the flowers are irregular and the fruit is never angled.

### LOBSTER CACTUS

The true *Zygocactus truncatus,* aside from its characteristic flower and berry, does closely resemble a Schlumbergera, but the margins of its joints have sharp teeth, rather than the rounded crenations, and two prominent claws at the otherwise blunt joint tips. These claws give rise to the appropriate name, "Lobster Cactus." Claw or Crab Cactus are other names used. If you possess a plant of this description, regardless of whether it blooms toward the end of the year or not, do not call it Christmas Cactus but rather Lobster Cactus. As mentioned previously, the Zygocactus flowers show a great variation in color; consequently, nearly a hundred forms have been mentioned in early day literature. However, since only meager descriptions accompanied these names, it is difficult to trace their history in these modern times. It is possible that many of the forms have been lost or gone out of circulation. We know, too, that the blooming season for both Zygocactus and Schlumbergera varies considerably. Some forms begin to flower as early as October and some as late as May. A few years ago I had one Schlumbergera blooming in July, when normally it bloomed in December and January.

Whether these epiphytic cacti bloom for Thanksgiving, Christmas, or Easter, their culture is not difficult. Keep in mind that they are jungle inhabitants and, as such, prefer richer soil mixture of humus and leaf mold. Keep the plants moist but not soggy, place outdoors in summer in a shady location where air circulation is good, and give the necessary rest in early fall and another after the flowering period. When buds are forming, the plants should be watered more often but not overhead. Moving the plants about and air drafts might cause bud drop, and therefore precautions should be taken. If a normal rest period is not given, few, if any, flowers can be expected.

Zygocacti and Schlumbergeras need not be transplanted often. A plant can be kept in the same container for several years if the drainage is perfect, the soil light and loose, and plant food—not too rich in nitrogen content—given in season.

### CHIAPASIA

*Chiapasia Nelsonii* is another very good window plant and preferably a hanging pot subject. In character it resembles a dwarf Epiphyllum. The growth is erect at first, composed of small, flat, slightly notched stems about an inch broad. Numerous canes arising from the base subsequently branch out, giving the plant a more fragile appearance than any of the other "leafy" unarmed cacti. When grown under proper conditions it has surprisingly good lasting qualities. The attractive plant grows wild in the State of Chiapas (Mexico), from which it derives its generic name. The small but very attractive blossoms of lilac pink appear on the lateral branches in early spring. They are lily-like, tubular at the base, and flattening out above like a morning-glory, with the pistil and stamens extending beyond the delicately tinted petals. The flowers measure two inches in diameter. Because of the shape of the flowers this cactus is beginning to be called "Morning Glory Cactus." The Chiapasia has now been crossed with some of the small-flowered Epiphyllums, and some outstanding hybrids are in the trade.

### DISOCACTUS AND OTHER GENERA

Disocactus is another irregularly branching, spineless cactus allied to Chiapasia. Although it was introduced into England as early as 1839, it is uncommon in collections. Two species only are known to exist—namely *Disocactus biformis* and *D. Eichlamii,* the former from Honduras and the latter from Guatemala. Disocactus produces cylindrical stems from which grow many flattened, leaf-like joints. Small, unspectacular, slender, tubular flowers with few, long, extremely narrow petals appear in the uppermost areoles being magenta to bright red in color.

*Nopalxochia phyllanthoides,* dating back to 1651, is reputedly one of the oldest known species of cacti. It has been used quite frequently in breeding, and many of the smaller pink flowered Epiphyllum hybrids contain blood of this interesting cactus. The plant is a rather bushy, thickly branched epiphyte suitable for basket culture. Its medium-sized flowers of pink, about four inches long, are borne copiously on the lateral areoles of the joints. The elusive *Epiphyllum Ackermannii,* from which many garden varieties have been obtained, has often been suspected of hybrid origin, but another one of my friends, Dr. Charles L. Gilly, collected it in a canyon in Vera Cruz near the town of Jalapa in 1943, thereby clarifying its status. Since the flowers of *Nopalxochia phyllanthoides* and *Epiphyllum Ackermannii* are very much alike, the two plants may be closely related, so it was proposed to include Ackermannii as a second species in Nopalxochia. In 1947, Tom MacDougall described a third species which he called *Nopalxochia Conzattianum.* It was found to be fairly common at Santiago Lachiguiri in Oaxaca, where it grows on trees. The flowers were bright red with orange suffusion. Cuttings were distributed in California but most of the stock was lost through unusual cold winters in recent years and it will be a long time before this plant will be available to the trade.

Now that I have dealt with most of the Epiphyllanae worthy of cultivation in your homes, let us turn to a number of other interesting plants that grow in the same environment. These are the Rhipsalidanae, mostly epiphytic cacti, much branched, usually spineless, with very small, often tubeless flowers. It is indeed difficult to explain to most people that its species are true cacti. There are a number of genera included in this subtribe, but I shall deal only with the few that are grown in collections and that can be purchased from dealers. Probably the best known are the Rhipsalis, and no window-sill gardener can go wrong by including a few of these in his choice house plants. Rhipsalis plants are of rather diverse form, some with slender cylindrical stems and others with flattened leaf-like joints. Although the flowers are rather tiny, they are produced in such profusion that a well grown plant covered with hundreds of miniature blossoms is a sight to behold! Oftentimes the flowers are followed by beautiful berries, resembling Mistletoe; and some growers have dubbed the plants "Mistletoe Cactus."

There are more than fifty species of Rhipsalis recognized by botanists today. They are confined to subtropic sections of the two Americas, the greater majority being found in southern Brazil and other parts of South America. One species has been collected in Florida (the only one in continental United States), and one or two in the Old World, in Madagascar, and Tropical Africa, where it is believed they may have been introduced by migratory birds. All kinds of theories are being advanced as to how these seemingly All-American cacti found their way across the ocean.

on trees. The flowers were bright red with orange suffusion. Cuttings were distributed in California but most of the stock was lost through unusual cold winters in recent years and it will be a long time before this plant will be available to the trade.

hanging pots or small wall baskets; but they will do well as potted plants
among a collection of such common house plants as begonias, geraniums,
and African violets. I have grown both the leaf-like and cylindric-
stemmed forms in the ground in our Cactus House, but they do best
when treated and grown like the Epiphyllums, in the same kind of soil
and under identical cultural conditions.

*Rhipsalis cassutha,* dating back to the eighteenth century, is the commonest and oldest species known. In the wild it starts as a modest leafless
plantlet on the trunk or branch of a giant tree. As it grows it produces
large clusters of wicker-work stems (that's what Rhipsalis literally means)
that may be ten feet or more in length. The slender light green stems
become dotted with small, white, star-shaped flowers and later by white,
glutinous berries reminiscent of the mistletoe plant.

A good many of the Rhipsalis species have the habit of *Rhipsalis cassutha.* About thirty of them possess cylindric or terete stems in various
degrees of thickness, length of branches and branchlets, as well as degrees of stoutness, flexibility, with or without bristles, and color of flowers and fruit. Among these the best are the following:

| | |
|---|---|
| *Rhipsalis capilliformis* | *Rhipsalis Lindbergiana* |
| *cassutha* | *lumbricoides* |
| *cereuscula* | *megalantha* |
| *cribrata* | *Neves-Armondii* |
| *dissimilis* | *puniceo-discus* |
| *gibberula* | *Shaferi* |
| *grandiflora* | *teres* |
| *heteroclada* | *virgata* |

*Rhipsalis capilliformis* probably presents the daintiest appearance. It is
composed of many short cylindrical stems forming an intricate network
of hair-like branches. The small, creamy blossoms are only a quarter of
an inch broad and are scattered along the sides of the branches, later
maturing into globose, pinkish fruits. Another of the delicate branched
species is *Rhipsalis heteroclada,* producing branches in verticillate clusters
and bearing white flowers and white fruits.

*Rhipsalis grandiflora,* a stout-stemmed form, is prominent as it has branches of pencil thickness upon which half-inch long cream-colored blossoms are scattered. The largest flowered member is *Rhipsalis megalantha,* whose blossoms are fully one and a half inches across. It was found on an island off the coast of Brazil.

*Rhipsalis Neves-Armondii,* in my estimation, is one of the showiest. It starts to bloom in early November, at which time its lemon-like fragrance permeates the air in its immediate vicinity. The blossoms bear a striking resemblance to the flowers of *Pereskia aculeata,* which is regarded as the most primitive member of the Cactus family. *Rhipsalis Neves-Armondii* is composed of many cylindric stems from the ends of which grow the short terete branches in whorls of three to ten. The area around the tiny areoles is usually purple tinted. The flowers are borne near the tips of the branches and are sessile, seeming to burst out through the epidermis. The epidermal wall splits into four very short sepal-like, membranous appendages around the perianth and might be mistakingly taken for sepals, although the "lobes" have no connection with the flower.

There is another group of Rhipsalis whose stems are usually heavier and angled or ribbed rather than terete. They also branch and rebranch profusely. According to the species the stems can be three-angled as in *Rhipsalis trigona,* five-angled as in *Rhipsalis pentaptera,* and the angles can be very prominent or faint and even indented. *Rhipsalis paradoxa* is the oddest and most whimsical of the lot. It produces zigzag links and, as Cactus Pete suggests, "look pinched as if made from pottery clay by human fingers." This one is appropriately called "Chain Cactus."

Still another group is altogether foreign to any of the above shapes. The erect to pendant branches are either narrow or broad, thin or thick, short or elongated, but always flattened and leaf-like. Their margins are nearly entire or, in many instances, strongly and deeply crenate, and even wavy. In shape the branches can be oblong to elliptic, orbicular to rhombic, and even lance-shaped. In color the branches are glossy green to dull green, often becoming red when grown in sunlight.

*Rhipsalis Houlletiana,* in my estimation, is one of the most graceful of the leafy types, its long arching stems often reaching more than three feet in length. The small yellowish-white flowers are borne abundantly from the marginal areoles, later followed by round, carmine-red fruit. *Rhipsalis crispat*a is a very desirable species of upright or slightly arching growth. The broad stems are fairly stiff, wavy along the margin and roundish in shape, producing yellowish blossoms from the areoles.

*Rhipsalis mesembryanthemoides* should not be overlooked because of its fancied resemblance to a totally unrelated South African fig marigold. It is a much branched, pale-green bushy plant, thickly adorned with small terete branches on the main stems unlike any other Rhipsalis in existence. It flowers profusely at areoles of the branchlets.

### HARIOTA

Closely allied to Rhipsalis are the Hariotas. *Hariota salicornioides* is the outstanding member. It is composed of many clavate or bottle-shaped branchlets supporting small but showy golden yellow flowers. It should be included in every collection.

### PSEUDORHIPSALIS

One other small genus of epiphytic plants with thin, flattened joints to be eagerly sought is Pseudorhipsalis. Only two species were known until Tom MacDougall discovered the best of them all on his collecting excursion to Mexico in the winter of 1939-1940. This one was subsequently named *Pseudorhipsalis macrantha* and is destined to become a great favorite with all cactus enthusiasts. The plant growth resembles many of the Epiphyllums and is unexcelled as a hanging basket subject. The flowers are many times larger than any Rhipsalis and are very fragrant with a definite slender inch-long tube topped by a perianth of nine to thirteen, long, very narrow yellow lobes.

CRYPTOCEREUS

This discourse on "Jungle Cacti" would be incomplete without the mention of a strange cactaceous plant that is destined to become a great favorite as soon as stock is worked up in quantity. MacDougall and I found it growing on a tree in a rain forest some twelve miles north of the Zoque Indian town of Ocozocoautla in Chiapas, Mexico. He had come across it a year earlier and distributed cuttings to several nurserymen on the West Coast. It resembles *Epiphyllum anguliger* and *Epiphyllum Darrahii* rather closely, but its relationship stops there. Its fishbone-shaped pads or joints are of thicker texture and carry tiny spines in the areoles. Its flowers are incomparable, being exceedingly showy and highly fragrant. They are about six inches long, rather thick textured and very colorful. The flower tube, scales, and outermost perianth segments are reddish purple, and the petals are creamy to white with a rather stout style exserted beyond the stamens and featuring long, stout, spreading stigma lobes. It has been christened *Cryptocereus Anthonyanus* and, because its flower is more Hylocereoid, it has been placed in subtribe Hylocereanae rather than in Epiphyllanae. It is very likely that hybridizers will resort to Cryptocereus for a new strain of horticultural varieties.

# CHAPTER III

# CARE OF CACTI AND DISEASES

**M**ANY PERSONS find great difficulty in managing cactus plants throughout the year. Plant lovers, especially those who are highly successful with other house plants, will usually run into a streak of bad luck when attempting to grow these fantastic members of the cactus tribe. The great error, of course, lies in the grower himself. Too often, plants of this type are given the same care as the geranium, the aspidistra, the philodendron, and the begonia. It never occurs to such a grower that cactus plants require care just the opposite of that generally given to ordinary house favorites.

There is also the idea that cacti need no attention whatsoever. To the contrary, even among cactus plants different cultural methods must be applied. Consider first the cacti that thrive under hot sun and in poor soil where the rainfall is scanty. Such plants would be utterly miserable in a humid atmosphere and eventually would succumb to kindness if given plenty of water. Then consider the forest and epiphytic cacti that shun the fierce rays of a tropical sun and welcome water and filtered light. Grow these plants under desert conditions and see how long they would last in your collection! In order to be successful with any kind of a plant one should acquaint himself with the conditions of the natural habitat.

Cacti that are very thick stemmed and very spiny usually hail from regions of adverse conditions, and they have developed the ability to take up and store within their stems the moisture which at intervals comes their way. They have also developed a spiny armament which acts as a shield against the scorching rays of the sun. Cacti that fall into this class make an excellent subject for our homes, especially where hot and dry conditions exist in living rooms. They require a minimum of care. Such plants are found in the genera Echinocactus, Echinocereus, Ariocarpus, Astrophytum, Sclerocactus, Ferocactus, Melocactus, and their close relatives.

On the other hand, the flat, thin-stemmed, and slenderly terete branched cacti give a hint that they require a richer soil and more humid surroundings and would be suitable for sun rooms and screened porches. These types are found in Epiphyllum, Zygocactus, Rhipsalis, Schlumbergera, Selenicereus, Aporocactus, Chiapasia, Pereskia, and many others, most of them characterized by the absence of spines or, when these are present, they are usually scant, short, and more or less flexible.

The active season for most cacti begins in March or even earlier, depending upon the species and in what part of the country they are being grown. In the Middle West, around the St. Louis area, warm weather will often make its appearance in February, but freezing weather is possible up into late April. In the Chicago area and other points north, colder weather will prevail three to six weeks longer. On these warm days cacti can be placed temporarily outdoors to absorb the warm rays of sun and fresh air. This may not be too easy for those people living in apartments and those with large collections. The next best thing to do is to open the windows so that fresh air will get to the plants. By supplying air and sun in gradual degrees, the cacti are prepared to withstand the intense sunlight and heat later on in the season. If cold weather is predicted for the night, it would be wise to bring the plants indoors until the next warm spell or at least place a cover of burlap, cloth, or newspapers over the plants. In my estimation, even though the moving in and out of the plants may prove to be a task at this time, the cacti will repay you for this deed and you'll be able to enjoy them for a longer time.

Usually, during May, cacti can be set out permanently, either in rockeries, in beds, or in borders. Because of the heavy spring rains in our Middle West, cacti should be planted on a slope so that excess water will readily drain off. Although plants will do better if planted directly in the soil, the average worker will not have the time to dig them up carefully and repot them in the fall, so the pots should be plunged in the ground to within an inch of the rim and the surface covered with gravel, limestone chat, or other small rocks.

## WATERING

Cactus plants may be watered daily in the growing season, if the weather is fine; and they may be also syringed frequently. It is a mistake to believe that they can live without water. In fact, if good drainage is provided, the plants will stand a great deal of water and will thrive on it. Summer rains are often not sufficient to wet the soil of a pot plant thoroughly, so artificial sprinkling must be resorted to. However, rain water is very beneficial, and one good rain is better than several hose waterings. Cacti that are planted directly in the soil or their pots plunged in will not require as much watering as the potted plants set directly on the ground or on shelves. Exposed pots dry out quickly in continuous days of sunlight. The best time to water is early morning or late in the afternoon when the sun is not too strong. If watering is performed between the hours of 10:00 a.m. and 4:00 p.m., the plants may suffer sunburn or even be cooked. Drops of water adhering to the crowns, thorns, or hair will act as magnifying lenses for the sun rays during that period and some plants will suffer; so be cautious if you must water around that time of day. Plants that must be kept indoors during the summer will require watering daily if kept on sunny window sills or sun porches and if the containers are small and drainage is good. On dreary days watering can be dispensed with. A cursory examination of the pots will tell you whether daily watering is necessary. On some days I have watered the cacti both in the morning and evening; on others watering was sufficient for two days or even three. Get acquainted with the needs and you will better understand the plants that are giving you the enjoyment you seek.

To water or not to water during the dormant season is probably the most perplexing problem that faces the cactus grower. I believe that water should be given only when necessity dictates and then only in small quantities. Of course, this procedure must again depend upon the type and location of the resting place.

Cacti that spend their dormancy in greenhouses need not be watered as frequently as those kept in ordinary living quarters where the air is exceptionally dry. The moisture-laden atmosphere of greenhouses will suffice to keep such cactus plants greener and healthier in appearance and will likewise have a tendency to start their spring growth much earlier, even if no water is applied to them during the whole dormant season. Cacti given no moisture in warmer, drier surroundings of living rooms will become dry, dirty, paler in color, and often very withered. Such plants will take much longer to recuperate.

In my opinion, it is advisable to keep the soil a little moist rather than too dry. The golden rule to apply is to water sparingly and more frequently rather than to apply too much or to give too much after long lapses. Generally it is necessary to water about once every seven to ten days. When practicing this method it is wise to water from below by placing the pot in a saucer or pan of water and permitting the moisture to soak up. In doing this, never leave the container in water more than five minutes; otherwise the soil will become soppingly wet and this will do more harm than good at this season. When watering from above it is essential not to get any moisture on the plants, as evaporation is slow at this season and even a drop of water in the crown of the plant or on any other part of the cactus stem may be the starting point of a rot infection. An occasional syringing to wash away dirt that settles on the plants is advisable but the cleansing of the stems must be performed only on sunny days.

A note about watering cactus seedlings will not be amiss here. Cactus seedlings are apt to dry up more quickly than those of a more mature plant, and for this reason it is practicable to keep seedling pots slightly moist at all times, even in the dormant period. A suggestion is offered here to all seedling propagators who must winter their cacti in living rooms. A miniature greenhouse will be highly serviceable for small plants, because the air in it will be much more humid than in any ordinary room, and the small compartment will help to keep the tiny plants from being covered by flying dust. Many dealers are now offering these tiny glasshouses at reasonable prices, but if the cactus fancier has not the means to procure one, an improvised glass-box can be made readily and quite cheaply.

An aquarium, especially of the rectangular type, can also be utilized for the same purpose. All cacti in small pots can be placed in these glasshouses, setting the pots on peat moss or moist sand which will keep the plants moist for a long time. It isn't even necessary to water the soil of the pot if the peat or sand is kept uniformly moist. However, the small glasshouses must be ventilated frequently, because clean, fresh air is essential for the successful culture of all succulent plantlets.


## RESTING

Under natural conditions all plants in general are subject to a resting period. Mother Nature provides for this exigency by ushering in the winter season to suspend all growth in plants. In milder climates, where the temperature does not drop low enough to interrupt plant growth, it is the rainless season that again furnishes this urgent period. Cacti grown in cultivation also require a rest period. In order to duplicate the natural conditions during the winter or dormant season, it will be necessary to give some attention to the plants as regards temperature, light, watering, and air.

It is not essential to begin wintering cacti too soon, as this procedure will be unpropitious for the plants. Truly, the month of September sometimes tends to be cool with unfavorable weather predominating which has a tendency to suspend growth; but generally there are still enough sunny days to the end of October for the plants to grow, although not regularly. (Seasons below the equator are just the reverse of ours. For example, when we are enjoying summer the folks in Australia are having winter.) Even during the early part of November the weather may be mild enough to permit the cacti to remain outdoors. Experience has shown that the longer the cacti are left in their summer places, the better they will be able to survive the winter season. The cool autumnal nights are beneficial to most cacti since the lower night temperatures seem to promote the hardening and ripening of cactus stems. It is advisable, then, to leave most cactus plants outdoors until frost.

After the cacti have been brought indoors, they will continue to grow, and there is no need for an immediate rest for the plants. Watering should not be entirely suspended but greatly diminished and the plants gradually brought into the dormant state. Even if the resting period is begun in the early part of November with the cessation of water, these thorny plants will still grow, especially when the temperatures of their resting places are relatively high. The water that is stored in each plant body is sufficient to last the cactus for one or two months if not even a drop of water is applied to the ground.

Some attention should be given to a place where the cacti are being rested. The best places to winter cacti are cool cellars, verandas, sun porches, lighted halls, or any other compartments that are frost-free, comparatively dry and well-ventilated, and where there is plenty of light. In summing up the temperature problem it is found that cacti are best rested in a temperature of 45 to 50 degrees F.

Transplanting, when necessary, is to be done at the end of the dormant season, when new growth is beginning. A cactus need not be shifted unless it has outgrown its pot. Some species can remain in the same container for several years as long as a little fertilizer is applied during the growing season. If a plant is at a standstill for a long time, it is best to take it out of the pot and examine the root system, as the cause may lie there. Too often the roots have dried up or rotted away and the plant remains dormant even in the growing season. Always repot in fresh soil and provide adequate drainage.

## SOILS AND FERTILIZERS

Each grower usually has a preference for a soil mixture of his own. Each uses the basic materials in different proportions or with the addition of secondary ingredients with success. The formula consists of loam, leaf mold, and sand. Pulverized cow manure, bone meal, or some commercial fertilizer is often added in small quantities. I prefer to use a

4-12-4 formula rather than one with higher nitrogen content. This can be worked into the soil at the rate of one four-inch pot of fertilizer to a bushel of soil. Some of the large growers of cacti prepare their own cactus food and sell it to their customers. A well balanced fertilizer used according to direction helps a cactus to make a normal, matured, flowering growth. Don't try to overfeed your plants or they'll get indigestion. Jungle cacti, like the Epiphyllums, Zygocacti, and like can be fed weak, liquid manure or any of the foliar feeding compounds now on the market. These jungle inhabitants living above the ground certainly must derive a good deal of food from the air, and now the grower can supply it to the plants as naturally as Mother Nature does it in the outdoors. Frequently you may read that one application is all that is necessary for a plant to show remarkable results, but I have found that several applications are needed before good growth is noticeable. It is best to give light applications a little more often than a heavier application at one time. Follow the instructions of the manufacturer in the use of his product and be safe with your plants!

## INSECTS

A good cactus grower will make frequent inspections of his plants to detect any sign of insect life. Under cultivation in the home or greenhouse, far removed from the natural home of the cactus, relatively few of the natural cactus insects are likely to infest the plants. In 1912 the United States government made a study of cactus insects and found that there were 324 species associated with these prickly plants. However, there will be several common garden and greenhouse pests that will cause considerable annoyance in our pursuit of growing cacti. Chiefly, these insects are introduced into a cactus collection from other plants and ornamentals that are grown so extensively in greenhouses and homes. Hardly any cactus fancier can say his plants are free from insect attack, but a cactus collection can be kept surprisingly clean without much effort on the owner's part if a careful watch is maintained for the mischievous scamps and a judicious use of insecticides is resorted to. Such insects as the grasshoppers, caterpillars, and others mostly likely to be present in the flower garden will often get into a cactus bed or into a greenhouse through unscreened doors and ventilators and do considerable damage before a remedy can be applied for their control. Throughout the warm season, these voracious feeders may cause more or less continuous trouble especially upon the tender and juicy seedlings. The various tropical insects that thrive in our greenhouses, like the scales and mealy bugs, are usually difficult to control, but when once thoroughly eradicated from the cactus plants will not appear again until a newly infested plant is introduced among the healthy ones.

In order to check the spread of injurious insects it will be expedient to use insecticides that are especially designed for the killing of such pests. Primarily we must learn what type of "bug" is feeding upon our plants—whether it be a chewing kind, or one that sucks.

Those insects, possessing biting or chewing mouth parts, as the caterpillars, grasshoppers, and beetles that chew solid particles of food, can be controlled only by the use of stomach poisons or poisonous gases. The poisoned food must enter into their stomachs to do the work of eradication.

The sucking insects, like the aphids, mealy bugs, and other scale insects, are provided by nature with needle-like mouth parts that are used to pierce the plant tissues and to extract the juice from within. Poison on the surface of the plant will not affect such insects and, therefore, contact insecticides and poisonous gases will be needed to kill these pests. It is to be remembered that the sprays must come in contact with the body of the insect in order to be effective.

Arsenate of lead is probably the most widely used of stomach poisons and it can be used as a spray or a dust, as well as in poison baits. When using the spray about ten teaspoonfuls to a gallon of water are sufficient to kill most chewing insects. For use, it must be mixed in the proportion of one of arsenic to about nine parts of flour, talc, or hydrated lime. Paris green is another effective arsenical product and highly efficacious when used in poison baits. Of the contact insecticides, nicotine is probably the most popular. There are several other effective sprays manufactured under various trade names, Greenhouse Volck being particularly effective for the control of scale insects and red spider.

Perhaps the most persistent and most serious insect pests of the cacti in cultivation are the scale insects, in which group the mealy bugs are generally included. Other insects attacking cactus plants are aphids, thrips, grasshoppers, and several other well known greenhouse pests, but all of these are usually of minor importance, although sometimes any of these may cause considerable annoyance.

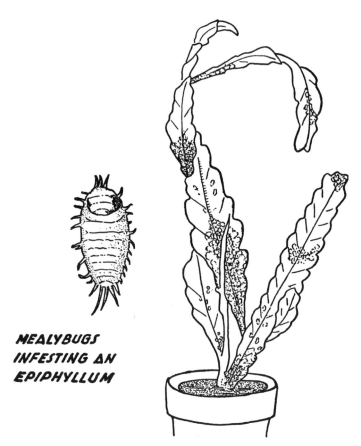

**MEALYBUGS INFESTING AN EPIPHYLLUM**

In the following paragraphs I shall consider those insects and other pests that are apt to be the direct or indirect causes of injury to cactus plants in the home or greenhouse and I shall also treat of various methods for their control.

*Mealy Bugs.* Of all the insects that use the cactus plant for a host, none are of such primary importance as the mealy bugs. Almost every variety of cactus is likely to be attacked by these cottony-covered insects. There are many species of mealy bugs, and hardly any greenhouse plant is free from their attack. The insects are easily identified because they cover themselves and their eggs with a white cottony substance and very often the beginner mistakes a colony for a fungus growth, so deceiving is their appearance. These destructive bugs usually congregate in protected places, as under the spines, in the grooves of new growth, and at the bases of joints, where they extract the juices from the cactus and cause injury in much the same manner as the scale insects.

The mealy bug, because of its peculiar structure and the rapidity of its reproduction, is one of the most difficult insects to control. The female has the ability to lay about 500 eggs which she secretes in a mass of cotton, eggs hatching out over a period of ten days under greenhouse conditions. In heavily infested greenhouses, several generations may be born yearly. The bugs do not move about very much, but usually restrict themselves to a certain area on a cactus joint. The mealy bug inserts its needle-like beak into the plant body and then sucks out the juice. The area heavily infested by these bugs will become lifeless, drab looking, and eventually will dry up. These bugs also give off a sweet secretion called honeydew, and the whole cactus is often covered by this sticky excretion in which a sooty, dirty-colored mold develops, causing a black discoloration on the stems which only a vigorous washing will remove. It seems that the pincushion cacti—Mammillarias, Coryphanthas, Escobarias, and Dolichotheles—as well as the hedgehogs, Echinocereus, suffer more from the mealy bugs than from other insects, and frequently the plants succumb because of the insect ravage.

When cacti are heavily infested with mealy bugs, it is advisable to hose off the infested plants with a strong spray of water. This method which is very effective because it knocks off the insects and washes off the sticky excrement left by the bugs, is heartily recommended, especially when the mealy bugs are congregated behind a very spiny armament and it is impossible for a contact insecticide to penetrate to their bodies. Where there is a large glasshouse, cyanogas fumigation can be practiced, but it will not kill all the bugs and it will not destroy the eggs.

*Root Louse.* This insect is similar to the mealy bug, although a trifle smaller and as devastating in its work as the latter. The dormant season affords an opportunity for the development and increase of the root louse and its presence is more dangerous than almost any other plant pest since this insect congregates about the roots, piercing the tender rootlets and sucking out the juices. The roots thus attacked will eventually dry up and, while in this condition, may be susceptible to rot diseases when water is applied.

Whenever a cactus looks sickly, it may be a good idea to take the plant out of the pot and examine the roots for this louse. If any white cottony masses are seen about the roots, shake off all soil from the roots, discard the soil, and dip the roots in a bath of denatured alcohol for about two minutes. After this operation, permit the plant to dry thoroughly before planting into a clean container, using fresh soil. Often a good wash in cold water will rid the plant of the root louse. In early March it may be a good idea to turn all plants out of the pot to see whether the roots are infected, for the root louse thrives in a dry soil and the dormant season is conducive for its procreation.

*Scale Insects.* Several varieties of scale insects are likely to infest cactus plants and are often very troublesome when permitted to multiply. These insects can be recognized by their more or less arched, thick and rigid, shell-like covering. Their favorite cactus seems to be the flat-jointed Prickly Pear, but the Zygocacti, Schlumbergeras, and Epiphyllums are also attacked. Often the bugs become so abundant that they practically cover the entire pad-like points. As these sucking insects withdraw large quantities of sap from the juicy Prickly Pears, the pads will become discolored and eventually drop off. If no remedy is applied, the whole plant may be lost. Spraying with a good contact insecticide will control the insects. Any good oil emulsion spray on the market will be satisfactory if applied according to the manufacturer's directions. A very good product known as Greenhouse Volck is one of the best oil emulsions for the control of scale insects on cactus plants, and very often one application is sufficient.

*Aphids.* These soft-bodied insects are very fond of the young tips of plants and sometimes will attack the new growths of such cacti as Hylocereus, Selenicereus, Rhipsalis, and Pereskias. The various species of plant lice vary in color and are slightly larger than a pinhead. They congregate in great numbers about the new growth or on the underside of Pereskia

leaves and feed by sucking the juices from the more tender portions of
the cactus plants. They frequently are seen on cactus flowers.

The aphids, like the mealy bugs, produce honeydew, a sweetish ex-
cretory substance, which is much sought after by ants. The lice reproduce
at a rapid rate and are active feeders, but it is hardly possible that they

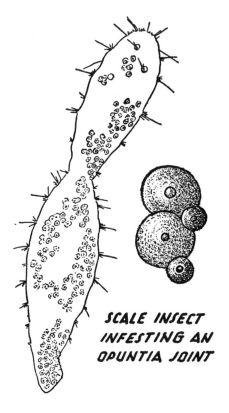

SCALE INSECT
INFESTING AN
OPUNTIA JOINT

would cause the death of a mature plant. Truly, the portion attacked by
these common garden pests will be seriously injured and the portion so
weakened is apt to become host to other diseases, so it is advisable to
get rid of them as soon as they make their appearance. Plant lice can
be easily controlled with a contact spray made up of one teaspoonful of
Nicotine (Black leaf 40) to a quart of water. The spray must touch the
bodies of the insects to smother them, if satisfactory results are to be

attained. If other insects could be controlled as easily as the aphids, there would be no need for further worry on the gardener's part.

*Red Spider.* This cosmopolitan, little, eight-legged mite is not a true insect, but it is one of the pests that may attack cactus plants. These tiny mites are so small that they are hardly perceptible to the eye, yet they can be observed to move about when disturbed. They are more

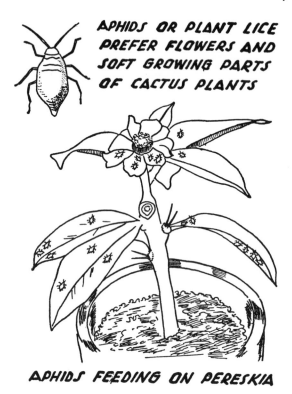

APHIDS OR PLANT LICE PREFER FLOWERS AND SOFT GROWING PARTS OF CACTUS PLANTS

APHIDS FEEDING ON PERESKIA

easily detected by their characteristic injury to the plants. The red spiders feed by piercing the new growth on such cacti as the Hylocereus, Seleni-cereus, Pereskia, etc., and then sucking the sap. The joints infested by these mites will be coated with silken threads spun in tent-like webs under which they live. The injured portions will assume a blotched, rusted appearance under the webs, greatly disfiguring the tender growths which ultimately may dry up. Sometimes a whole joint may succumb to the ravages of this pest. Seedlings often suffer from these infestations, especially if the plants are grown under hot and dry conditions.

In the greenhouse, red spiders breed all year round, only dull, moist weather being unfavorable to their development. Often these mites can be washed off the cacti with a strong spray of the hose, as the force of the water will knock the bugs to the muddy soil and they will be unable to crawl back to the plant. In the growing season, frequent syringing of the plants may be the only needed control. During the resting period, cacti may be attacked by red spiders, and the dormant season is conducive for their propagation. I have found Volck to be one of the best products for the control of red spider.

*Thrips.* The damage caused to cactus plants by these minute insects is not alarming, as they will attack only the seedlings and the injury will not, as a rule, prove fatal to the tiny succulent plantlets. Thrips usually attack such juicy vegetation as the Mesembryanthemums, Crassulas, and Kalanchoes from which they will pass onto the tender-skinned cactus seedlings, causing damage by rasping the plant tissues and leaving the attacked portion scarred and unattractive in appearance. These tiny insects may be brown or black and are somewhat quick in their motions. When disturbed the insect curves its abdomen up over its back (this is its characteristic motion preparatory to flight) and seemingly jumps for cover. Whenever thrips are noticeable on cacti, it will be wise to spray with a nicotine solution consisting of one-half ounce of Black leaf 40 to a quart of water. Any thrip hit by this efficient solution will die within two minutes.

*Ants.* These diligent workers of the insect world usually become very troublesome in a cactus collection, for they indirectly cause damage to cacti by the care they lavish upon aphids and scale insects, especially the mealy bugs. The ants are very fond of the delicious honeydew which these insects give off and, for the sake of this sweet excretion, they virtually succor those insects, carry them from one cactus to another, and thus aid in spreading the infestation.

Whenever any ants are detected crawling around plants, in the rock garden or greenhouse, it is a sure bet that plant lice and scale insects will be found in the collection. In the southern and midwestern states, the very active Argentine ant has become a serious greenhouse pest and a constant battle must be waged against it. I cannot recall a single instance where ants have been the direct cause of injury to cactus, but if these insects are found crawling up and down insect-free plants, it is only because of the sweet nectar that exudes from the buds and other parts of certain cacti.

The most successful control method for ants is the use of poison bait. There are several excellent products on the market for ant eradication—mostly syrup impregnated with arsenical poison. Just place a few drops of this poisoned syrup on a piece of stiff paper near an ant nest or in the ant path and next morning very few ants will be seen crawling around. A contact spray will rid the premises of the remaining stragglers. Nicotine is the best spray when used in the usual proportion of one teaspoonful to a quart of water.

Even more efficacious is a dust powder known as Chlordane. A single application will give effective control for several days. Chlordane may be purchased from any of the larger seed houses under the various trade name of Dow-Klor, Syn-Klor, Toxi-Chlor, etc. I have been using Dow-Klor,—40 per cent wettable, put out by the Dow Chemical Company, Midland, Michigan. Although it is claimed that this powder can be readily dissolved in water, to make a residual spray I have been using it only in the dust form. My compounding calls for one part of Dow-Klor to two parts of talc. The mixture is sprinkled in areas frequented by ants, particularly near cracks, bases of plants, or wherever the insects emerge.

Chlordane has a three-way action against insects. It serves as either a contact or stomach poison, and it gives off lethal fumes. A little of the powder placed at the base of a tree, vine support, or walls where ants are parading will cause them to drop, even without evidence of having touched the poison. When Chlordane is sprinkled on ant trains, the insects are paralyzed upon walking through the powder. Soon whole colonies are wiped out. Incidentally, Chlordane is also an effective control against cockroaches and other household pests.

*Grasshoppers.* These voracious feeders are not known to pass up a cactus collection, and I have seen considerable damage done by these jumping and flying pests. The cacti most likely to be attacked by grasshoppers are the Opuntias, Epiphyllums, Zygocacti, and Schlumbergeras.

Considerable portions will be chewed off, causing unsightly disfigurement; but the damage will be negligible compared to the injury that these insects may inflict upon cactus seedlings.

Grasshoppers usually gain entrance into greenhouses through unscreened ventilators and doors, and it will be wise for a greenhouse owner to screen these points of entrance for safety's sake. Whenever a grasshopper is noticed in the greenhouse, try to catch him, if possible, and trample under foot. Should these insects cause serious damage, it will be profitable to broadcast poisoned bran bait over the bench or on top of the soil in the pots. A formula compounded of 2½ pounds of bran, 2 ounces of Paris green, ½ pint of molasses or sugar syrup and mixed with 3 pints of water, will be very effective against grasshoppers, as well as cut worms, sow bugs, etc. Because Paris green is a very effective stomach poison, be careful to place the poisoned bait in places where other animal pets will not get at it.

*Sow Bugs.* These common greenhouse pests are not true insects, but relatives of the crabs and lobsters. They can be easily recognized, for when disturbed they roll themselves into a ball or pill—hence the name "pill bug" sometimes applied to them. In the greenhouse, the sow bug will usually be found in sheltered places where moisture is present, and outdoors they will be under cover in the rock garden or cactus bed. These minute crustaceans are scavengers, utilizing the decaying vegetable matter for food, but very frequently they will change their style of food and feed upon the tender stems of various cacti, especially if a rot injury appears at the base of a cactus. Oftentimes I have seen sow bugs attack a perfectly healthy joint of Opuntia and have watched them chew a hole through the joint or scoop out a cavity. As they are especially troublesome to small seedlings, it is of prime importance to get rid of the bugs. A poison bait, such as that used for grasshoppers, or one composed of nine parts of brown sugar to one part of Paris green, scattered about the benches, under pots, or on the soil will be instrumental in ridding the premises of these pests. Several prepared products are also obtainable on the market and can be bought from seed dealers and nurserymen. The cheapest method is to take a half of a potato, scoop out a cavity, and place the potato on the bench. Next morning you will notice all the pill bugs congregated in the hollow of the potato. Shake them off and squash them under foot.

*Millipeds.* These little animals which we are wont to call "thousand-leggers" are found commonly throughout the world, living in cool, damp places where there is an abundance of decaying organic matter. They feed mostly on vegetation in the decaying state, but they will frequently attack roots, and even stems and seedlings may suffer considerably. Seeds placed in the ground for germination are often singled out for their food.

The millipeds are often confused with centipedes, but the latter are usually found in cellars and frequently may crawl into living quarters. The centipedes have only one pair of legs to each body segment, are much faster in movement, and feed only on smaller animal life that they capture. The millipeds have two pair of legs to each segment and they are shorter in comparison. It is claimed that the thousand-leggers are responsible for disseminating certain bacterial and fungus organisms, so it will be our duty to rid the premises of these myriopods. The worms can be baited with a sliced potato dipped in Paris green solution or in arsenate of lead. Tobacco dust worked into the soil will give relief also.

*Other Insects.* Besides all the above pests, there may be a few more that may add trouble to the cactus fancier, but as a rule, some form of control will be found to check them. Often the individual grower works out some practical method to cope with the emergency.

A small louse is sometimes found in seedling pans and flats. These tiny insects move quickly in short jumps and have a habit of feeding upon the young rootlets of sprouted cacti. Almost any contact insecticide will destroy them, and often one dose will prove sufficient. Two or three moth balls placed in the seed pan with a cover glass over the seedlings is another efficient repellent.

## COMMON DISEASES

In the above paragraphs I tried to list the more common insect pests that generally attack cactus plants and the methods used to combat them. Now I'd like to deal with some of the common diseases which often plague cactus collections, causing the plants to become sickly, crippled, or dying specimens.

The most dreaded disease, believe it or not, is the rot disease. There are several types of this disease brought on by fungi in some cases and by faulty culture in others. It can attack the stem or start at the roots where it won't be suspected for some time until considerable damage has been done. The disease may be attributed to a number of causes. A bruise of any kind may start an infection. Faulty and prolonged watering may be another cause. When cacti are dried off too completely, the roots will die and if water is applied in heavy doses, rot will often set in, eventually working its way up into the stem if not checked. The disease also makes its entry when the soil is kept soggy, for cactus plants despise "wet feet."

*Root rot* often can be detected in the wilted and often discolored appearance shown in a plant that has fallen a victim to this dreaded disease. That is why a daily inspection of your collection is advised, for then you will get an idea which plants are faring well and which are not. A plant that shows no growth for a long time or starts to shrivel under supposedly good care should be taken out of its pot and examined for dead or rotted roots. The diseased roots must be cut off well above the rot, dried in the sunlight and then planted in sand or fresh sandy soil. If, however, the rot has reached the tissues of the stem, surgery must be performed well into the healthy stem. All infection must be removed if the disease is to be checked. Dusting with sulfur is advisable. Should the cutting instrument—whether a saw, knife or razor blade —be passed through the infected tissue it is advisable to sterilize the implement before making the final cut. If very little of the healthy portion of the plant remains after cutting, it is best to use it as a scion for grafting rather than a cutting for the sandbox.

In order to avoid rot diseases the simplest remedy is to supply the plant with the proper porous soil which will take a thorough watering before the next application is given. Also be careful that no bruises befall the plant, either in handling or pruning it, as a broken tissue is a source of possible infection, especially when the plant is not able to build up scar tissue quickly as in moist atmosphere.

*Black rot* is the name applied to a rot disease caused by a fungus entering a skin break usually near the base of a cactus. The skin break may be caused by insect injury. Black rot, as the name implies, turns living tissue into a soft mushy black mass which will spread inward rapidly if not checked. Scoop out the diseased tissue with a sharpened teaspoon which I find is far better than the blade of a knife. Keep water away from the wound until a hard scar is produced.

*Black spot* is another type of rot disease caused by fungus entering wounds on a cactus stem but, instead of being mushy, it is quite hard in texture. It frequently appears on Cereus stems where it is localized and does not, as a rule, spread out widely because the surrounding cells wall off the disease. All it does is disfigure the plant.

*Damp-off* is a common fungus disease prevalent in seed flats or pans, where the seedlings are too crowded, exceptionally moist, and kept in a close atmosphere. Seeds that are not cleaned properly of adhering pulp often bring on this disease. A disinfectant, like Semesan, will prevent "damping off."

*Green moss* and *algae* may develop on the soil surface or on a flower-pot. This may be due to fertilizer in the soil or too much moisture in the containers. Since this low form of plant life shuts out air and has a tendency to sour the soil, it impedes the growth of seedlings and contributes to root rot. Powdered charcoal sprinkled over the soil surface is a beneficial remedy to apply. Stirring the topsoil occasionally with a stick —a mild form of cultivation—will also prevent the formation of algae.

Occasionally tips of cacti may dry up or a corky tissue will discolor the stems. Nothing can be done about this. The cactus itself will fight the disease and wall-off the infected portion to keep it from spreading. As soon as the cactus checks it and the dried portions are really dry they can be usually knocked off easily. Of course, a permanent scar will remain.

Frequently *rust* may attack a cactus plant, especially during a long rainy spell in summer. In the greenhouse this condition may also be produced by overhead sprinkling of certain plants. The rust fungus causes a rust-brown appearance on Echinocereus, Mammillaria, Trichocereus, Lobivia, and other thin-skinned cacti injuring the epidermis and impairing the breathing apparatus of these plants. As a result the cacti will be disfigured and in some cases will shrivel up. Avoid sprinkling these cacti overhead for a long time and give them all the sunlight and fresh air possible. If new growth emerges and becomes sufficiently large for a cutting to be made, do it by all means and throw the diseased portion away.

# CHAPTER IV

# USES OF CACTI

## DESERTARIUMS

EVER SINCE 1930 when the liking for desert plants seized me, I began thinking seriously about experimenting with cactus plants in glass cases. When our first-born began to toddle on the kitchen floor, there was great danger of him coming in contact with the vicious thorns of prickly cacti that had been kept on window sills and on various tables around the windows. Not only that, but even my wife had often come in contact with the plants in her daily performance of household chores by brushing against them and often the spiny cacti would hook on her dress and unceremoniously eject themselves from the container. Then and there it was decided that some other method of practicing my hobby would have to be resorted to if peace and safety were expected to reign in our home. At the Missouri Botanical Garden I had already begun to experiment with terrariums and enjoyed a certain amount of success with them.

Glass gardening is not a new fad, having been in vogue for more than a century. However, cacti in such containers had been completely disregarded until about a quarter century ago. Glass cases have been used by botanical institutions and commercial growers for a long time in the transportation of plants between countries. It was Dr. Nathaniel Ward, a London physician, who first utilized glass containers for gardening purposes and ever since these glass gardens have been called Wardian cases in his honor.

The first Wardian cases were crude affairs; but today these miniature greenhouses—for that is exactly what they have come to be—may be purchased in any number of sizes and shapes, or they can be made at home with little trouble and expense. Old fish aquariums, clear glass candy and cracker jars, and various other glass containers make suitable gardens-in-glass.

Although woodland and jungle plants were originally used in the terrariums there was no reason why denizens of desert places could not be grown in them also. Thus the word "desertarium" was coined by me for these glass-enclosed gardens for cacti and succulents. A desertarium, as a house decoration, can hardly be surpassed.

How can anyone go about making a glass garden? Simply choose a suitable container of clear glass construction with smooth top edges so that a square of glass will fit nicely on it. For the beginner a small rectangular aquarium is most satisfactory, because the large opening permits the use of both hands in arranging and planting the miniature desert. Next in favor are the drum-shaped aquaria which are available in three practical sizes and are reasonable in price. Since they have a smaller opening, they may prove clumsy and some measure of patience and dexterous manipulation is required to create a picturesque desert landscape, although it can be done with practice. An advantage of the drum-shaped aquaria is that several will fit snugly on any window sill, which is an ideal location for these cases, since they will require all the light possible, especially during the drab winter season. Because they are easy to handle, they will not interfere with the busy housewife's regular duties.

Drainage is of the utmost importance in the growing of cacti in desertariums, and often this oversight is the cause of quick decay of many plants. Adequate drainage necessitates the use of porous soil and about a one-inch layer of sand or gravel (gravel preferably) at the bottom of the container. Several pieces of charcoal are added on top of the drainage material to prevent the soil from becoming sour, or powdered charcoal can be liberally mixed with the soil to keep the soil sweet.

Since soil will show unattractively through the glass, either paint the outside with aluminum paint or line the walls with sphagnum and other ordinary woodland moss to the intended depth of the soil level, remem-

bering to face the mossy side to the glass. A mixture of porous soil is then added and packed against the sides and bottom to a usual depth of about three inches or more, depending on the container and the plants to be grown in it. Rich loam is to be avoided for desert plants. Instead use a mixture of sand, well rotted leaf mold, and ordinary loam from your backyard or lot.

Several pieces of roughly eroded rock provide a background against which cacti are planted. Don't permit the rocks to be more prominent than the plants. Cacti can be arranged according to the individual's taste, but some really effective desert scenes may be worked out after examining a few desert pictures in popular magazines. With a little thought and patience, anyone can create an interesting terrarium—one that will bring joy to the creator and likewise excellent praise from friends. A miniature ten-cent store Mexican, with perhaps a thatched hut and burro figurines, can be added as an attraction. Other meaningless ornamentation should be avoided. Often well-placed stones for large boulders and mountains need be the only trimmings in a cactus-planted Wardian case.

Do not crowd the plants as in typical woodland or jungle garden. Care should be exercised in choosing small plants or those that are of slow growth. Although a terrarium can be entirely planted with cacti, the use of other dainty succulents will add a distinct charm. Of particular interest are the small rosettes of Haworthia that can be used to simulate century plants so typical of the American desert.

After all plants have been pressed into the soil, it is a good idea to cover the surface of the soil with sand or fine gravel, making sure that enough of this material lies at the base or around the plants to act as a protection against rot diseases. Finally, clean the inside glass as carefully as the outside, and remove any dirt, sand, or gravel that adheres to the plants with a small brush.

If care was exercised during the planting and no apparent injury caused to the root systems, the desert garden may be moistened lightly, primarily to settle the soil. If in doubt, refrain from water until three or more days have elapsed so that all bruises, whether on roots or stems, will have had sufficient time to heal over. When all operations are completed, place the terrarium where it will receive an abundance of light, for this is the chief requisite for success. In the evenings these containers may be placed in conspicuous places in the home, such as on mantels, pianos, end tables, or wall niches, where they are sure to attract deserved attention, especially if they can be lighted. The top should be partly covered with a square of glass slightly larger than the container opening and only removed when too much moisture within threatens to destroy the plants.

Watering the terrarium should pose no problem. It can be applied in sparing quantities no oftener than once or twice during the month. Some of my cases have gone waterless for several months and the cacti have thrived.

During the summer season the glass cover can be fitted tightly over the opening in order to create a "sweat" which will prove highly beneficial for the plants. This procedure can be performed once or twice weekly without any deleterious effects. Often this "sweat bath" during the summer period will be sufficient to provide all the moisture needed for weeks. If water must be applied it should be done in moderation. This will depend largely on the room temperature and the care given the Wardian cases. If rooms are excessively hot and dry, the plants inside the terrarium may require more moisture. If it is noticed that moisture lingers for long intervals around the plants, remove the lid and permit the soil to dry out before replacing the cover. This procedure should be attended to strictly, especially during the cloudy winter months when there is much danger of losing the plants through rot. Refuse to allow mold to develop. Mold may creep into the terrarium in several ways, but often the contributing factors are too much dampness and poor circulation of air. Infected parts should be immediately removed and sulfur applied to check the mold.

Light and fresh air are two important factors in the successful management of desertariums, and without them failure would surely follow. Unlike a woodland case, the desertarium exacts plenty of light, making a window sill the ideal location. Sun rooms and other well-lit compartments are also perfect quarters. To insure ventilation, see that the piece of glass serving as the cover over the opening does not set intact. Always leave about an inch or two of space open except during the "sweating" bath.

Desertariums require very little care once planted. The plants can be left alone for months at a time and still prosper. I have already experienced the thrill of utterly forgetting about the plants for long periods and finding them healthy and thrifty. On occasion I have applied water only two or three times during the whole year and often left the cases without any care whatsoever during the vacation absences with no resultant harm to the plants.

Almost any cactus, with the possible exception of the shrubby and viny

Pereskias, can be utilized for desertariums. Truly, a good number can be used only in the seedling stage; otherwise they are too bulky and obtrusive in the miniature settings. Whenever possible, seedlings of two- to five-inch proportions will fit into the scheme far better than the taller, often clumsier cuttings. The Pereskia group is to be entirely avoided, since even in seedling stages they grow too rank and fast for the glass desert. The Opuntia group features the flat-jointed Prickly Pears and the cylindric Chollas, many of which are suitable and lend that "deserty" touch to the terrarium. Sprigs of the Christmas-berry cactus, *Opuntia leptocaulis,* a slender shrubby cholla of our Southwestern deserts, thrives well in glass gardens, and unrooted cuttings need only be placed in the soil to take hold.

In my opinion, Mammillarias or Pincushion cacti are excellent subjects for the desertarium. There are more than three hundred recognized species, most of which are rather slow growers. Pincushion is an apt name for these cacti because most of them are globular to cylindrical in shape, characterized by nipples or tubercles in spiral rows, the apex of each nipple producing a spine or a cluster of spines—the whole remindful of a typical pincushion. The spiny armament is snowy-white or golden-yellow, reddish, blackish or gray. Sometimes the spines are so closely interlocked that they hide the body of the plant; and then in others the spiny pattern represents a diadem of stars. A few are copiously woolly and hairy.

Another satisfactory group that does exceedingly well in glass gardens is Echinopsis, commonly known as Easter Lily Cactus. Most of the species produce offsets, often in a tight cluster. The plant bodies are globular, more robust than the Mammillarias and, instead of tubercles arranged in spiral rows, they produce ribs outlined in youth with closely spaced areoles bearing slender spines.

Any of the arborescent Cerei in the juvenile stage can be used to overshadow the dwarf globular kinds just mentioned. The Cerei are usually slender at the base but fatten up above and can be used to represent the unique Saguaro, which is usually referred to as the "king of cacti" because of its towering proportions. In my opinion it is highly desirable to use cacti of various heights in the desertarium to create a more naturalistic effect. Try a desertarium in your home. You'll like it.

## DISH GARDENS

Dish gardens fascinate everyone. Cacti lend themselves admirably for this purpose as they require a minimum of care. I wouldn't be a bit surprised if many a cactophile first didn't get interested in these bizarre plants through a planted dish garden given to him by a friend; and, if not, either he viewed it in some floral shop window or saw examples at a flower show. Most florist shops have had great success in selling attractive cactus gardens. The trouble with some florists is that they like to slap together a few succulents in a dish filled with only sand or sphagnum moss; or they mix together plants that are unwholly suited to each other, such as a common Chinese evergreen or Dieffenbachia with a cactus. The former loves moisture, the latter thrives without it. Anyone buying such a garden will not become a potential customer because the plants, as a rule, will either dry up or rot, as the case may be. Some florists also have a tendency to overcrowd a bowl, believing that a well-filled dish will appeal to the eye. There may be something to the idea; but a simple garden, planted with artistic taste, will assure more satisfied customers.

The people who love bizarre plants but cannot grow them in small homes or apartments because of lack of space need not altogether be denied the pleasure of their company. Here is where the dish gardens will fill the need. They are easy to manage as they can be moved about at will when housecleaning is in order. There is also the fascination for those who wish to create pictorial arrangements; and too, it is surprising what fine assortment of desert jewels can be grown together in a small bowl.

For a dish garden, any flat dish made of glazed ware or metal can be used. The container should be quite shallow, about two or three inches deep, and may be of any shape and size, but the most popular dishes are from ten to fourteen inches across. A natural container, like a seashell, cactus wood skeleton, or cypress knee, that holds a handful or two of soil can be attractive.

The first step after a suitable container is chosen is to cover the bottom of the dish or bowl with a layer of gravel. Add a mixture of good porous loam, composed of equal parts of well rotted leaf mold, sand, and ordinary yard soil. A few chips of charcoal should be added to the soil or placed on top of the gravel to keep the soil sweet. Firm the soil with the fingers so that the dish is about half full. Some idea of the exact design of the garden should be had. It is well to put rocks into position when the dish is half full and press more soil tightly round them. Rocks simulate actual habitat conditions and often help in anchoring the plants in the shallow containers. A center of interest should be maintained, with proper enclosure on the back and sides by means of larger rocks and plants.

The planting of the dish garden is, of course, a matter of individual taste. However, some knowledge of related plants should be had and simplicity should be the rule. Never overcrowd the bowl with too many kinds of plants. Some florists frequently do this to create immediate sales, knowing full well that a crowded container holds a certain appeal to many buyers.

If you should be the recipient of a dish garden from a florist who has used desert material with jungle subjects, it is advisable to remove the unsuited plants and make it either into a true cactus and succulent garden that will require infrequent waterings, or turn it into a jungle garden that must be watered more often. There is no other choice for success.

Seedling or dwarf plants should be used in the plantings. Your local cactus dealer can supply you with inexpensive plants which are better than the higher priced rarer varieties. It is perfectly all right to use other succulents with the cacti, but I prefer to utilize cacti alone in a planting whenever possible. It might be to your advantage to stock up a few plants for replacements either by additional purchase or through your own propagations. A number of small cacti produce offsets readily, and others produce adventitious shoots when the parent stock is heavily cut.

After the plants are arranged, spread some gravel, sand, or limestone chat upon the surface of the soil. Do not water until the second or third day and after that only when the soil becomes dry. Colored sand is used frequently by the florist—I suppose to create a painted desert scene—but I prefer regular pea gravel or limestone chat.

On occasion, especially during the hot summer season, the planted dish garden can be submerged in a bathtub to receive a thorough watering.

CACTI DO WELL IN NOVELTY CONTAINERS

CACTUS ARRANGEMENTS ARE LONG LASTING

This should be done only when the gardens have dried out. Sometimes the little water that is supplied by overhead method is insufficient for the plants' needs. It is to be remembered that watering is the trickiest part in any kind of gardening, and only vigilant watch with experience will teach one how best to water the various plants. Learn to use the growing tip of the plants as a barometer. It is not wise to pour water directly on the plants, but an occasional syringing on warm days keeps them fresh and clean. This is likened to a shower bath you take to refresh your body. Make it a practice not to syringe a plant on a damp cloudy day or while the sun is beating down on it. In the former case, water may linger too long on the plant body and may induce a rot infection; in the latter, drops of water may act as a magnifying glass and cause a burn.

A well-executed dish garden will excite admiration and interest. After becoming adept at fixing these gardens, some really worthwhile artistic deserts can be created. A well placed rock or two and a few figurines are all that are needed to add mood to the miniature desert. One lady in our local cactus club, whose exhibits were always winners, used to make effective figurines out of regular dough which she kneaded and shaped, allowed to dry, and then painted. A little ingenuity goes a long way.

## NOVELTY CONTAINERS

The average person in his home seems to prefer glazed pots to ordinary flowerpots. In one way the bright colors are pleasing to the eye and seem to fit well with color schemes in the home. At the same time they need only be wiped occasionally with a damp cloth to keep them looking bright at all times. Novelty containers, too, are certainly attractive but not always the best for the plants. Oftentimes containers in the shape of fruits, vegetables, fish, and animals are made to accommodate only a thimbleful of soil, so that at best the plantings must be considered of short duration, although it is surprising the amount of abuse these will stand. Once I planted a seedling Selenicereus in a glazed cat novelty container that held less than a pinch of soil. The cactus grew for two years, attaining a foot in length and finally toppled from the shelf and broke off. It will surprise you what tenacity cactus plants possess!

Since most of the glazed pottery does not possess a drainage hole at bottom it must be remembered to drill a hole or at least place a layer of gravel at the bottom as is done for dish gardens. The soil will not dry out as fast as in an earthen flowerpot, and therefore water must be applied carefully in order that the soil does not become stale. I usually place the glazed containers in a sink and give them a thorough watering every two to three weeks without any apparent harm to the plants. Many of our local cactus club members grow their plants in novelty containers placed on window sills and on glass shelves built into the window. What could be more attractive?

## BUTTON GARDENS

Button gardening is comparatively a new fad and is another use to which cacti can be adapted. This is predominantly a ladies' hobby; but children as well as men can get a great thrill out of it, particularly convalescents in hospitals. Because cactus plants are plump with stored water, they can live for a long time without even being planted. It may take weeks before some of the chubby cuttings begin to dry up and die. Often cactus stems will start to sprout roots and attempt to grow because of humidity in the air. I have even seen blossoms appear on cactus that was left lying about on shelves for long periods.

Button gardens are literally dish gardens in miniature. Naturally they will not last as long, but many will look attractive for as long as six months. Button gardens are chiefly used as favors at parties. Garden clubs, too, often use this as a project for teaching shut-ins to pass their lonely hours. Ladies from a local garden club used to pay weekly visits to the veterans' hospital and teach patients how to make and care for these novelties. It helped to pass the hours and bring enjoyment to the men confined to beds.

Any kind of buttons can be used and tiny slips of cacti and other succulents glued to them or held in place with modeling clay. Large coat buttons serve as excellent bases for miniature scenes on which tiny figurines and colorful rocks can be used. Tips of colorful sedums, single leaves of Crassula, Kleinia, and other succulents, according to scale, and "pups" from clustering cacti are most frequently used. The moisture stored in the tiny plants will enable them to live on for many weeks. There is no need for watering, since the plants are full of moisture and will live several weeks before showing signs of deterioration.

The larger the button—and some of the coat buttons are really big— the more plants can be accommodated. In fact, some really artistic desert scenes can even be created with cacti alone. One of the finest cacti for button gardens is *Mammillaria elongata,* known to many as Lady Fingers cactus. It is a clustering cactus with slender stems about the thickness of a lady's dainty finger covered with a lacy pattern of bright golden, harmless spines. The plant branches freely from the base. Another attractive species is *Mammillaria prolifera,* somewhat similar to the former but covered with white bristles and bristle-like to fine hair-like spines. As its name implies, it also clusters prolifically. Still another miniature pincushion excellent for this purpose is *Mammillaria fragilis,* also prolific and of very dwarf growth. Other satisfactory cacti to be recommended are the Echinopsis, Rebutias, and Chamaecereus. These will last longer in button gardening than the other tender succulents.

Button gardens prepare aspirants for the flower arrangement art, as button gardens can be likened to flower arrangements on a diminutive scale. Master them, and then you can attempt larger and more elaborate pieces.

## CACTI ARRANGEMENTS

Artistic flower arrangements are always striking and enhance our homes considerably. Formerly only flowers were used for table pieces, mantel decorations, clubrooms, and breakfast nooks, but gradually colorful foliage, vegetables, fruits, and even dried material came into common usage. Cacti and succulents were overlooked, despite the fact that they held several advantages over the aforementioned materials. Cut succulents can live for a long time without water, and some of them can be handled quite roughly. Gradually a few pioneers began to use the sansevierias and aloe leaves for backgrounds, and then colorful rosettes of hen-and-chicken plants appeared as focal points. Later on, cacti in the form of Opuntia and Nopalea pads were used, and globose heads of Homalocephala, Mammillaria, and the like were bravely brought in to supplement them.

There are several advantages in using cacti and the other succulents in arrangements. One is that cuttings can last without water for a long time. They can be taken apart after the particular novelty has served its purpose, the stems rooted and grown again as potted plants. You cannot do this with flowers and nonsucculent material.

To make arrangements, shallow bowls, needle-like holders, and non-hardening modeling clay should be at your disposal. Succulent cuttings of different heights are then pressed onto the needle holder which is fastened to the bottom of the container with the clay. The holder and base of stems are covered with rocks, colored glass, gravel, soil, or plant material. Figurines oftentimes complete the composition. Almost any succulent lends itself well to arrangements and can be used with flowers, as well as with other nonsucculent material. The plants will remain lovely for several weeks, or until you're tired of the arrangement and then they can be potted for the window garden.

It is not always necessary to employ the prickly cacti in arrangements, although I admit that heavily spined kinds often impart that certain something to the completed piece. When using the wickedly armed Chollas or the spine cushioned Prickly Pears, be sure to handle the joints with a pair of ice-cube tongs or similar instrument. The Opuntias are probably the most treacherous specimens to deal with, but they look wonderful in an arrangement. Not all the Opuntias are wickedly armed; among them are several spineless or nearly spineless forms that can be handled quite freely. Although it must be remembered that all possess the glochids, these are sometimes submerged as in the Beaver Tail, *Opuntia basilaris*. Excellent Prickly Pear subjects are *Opuntia elata, O. macrartha, O. inamoena,* and *O. ficus-indica.* Spineless cacti include such well known subjects as *Astrophytum asterias, A. myriostigma, Ariocarpus fissuratus, A. Kotschoubeyanus, A. trigonus, Lophophora Williamsii* in what can be classed as the globose to flat-topped forms, and Epiphyllums, Schlumbergeras, Zygocactus, and Rhipsalis in the elongated leaf-like shapes.

## CACTI OUTDOORS

Thus far, I have mentioned cacti in indoor culture only, but it might surprise you to learn that these plants lend themselves admirably to outdoor beds also. Let's consider a small rockery. When neatly planned, such a garden will add new interest and pleasure to the homeowner's enjoyment of his grounds. In the planning and construction of a rockery, several facts should be borne in mind: whether it be strictly a cactus garden, a mixture of other succulents, or a combination of alpines and succulents. After the type of rockery has been decided, consideration must be given to the site, the size, exposure, and general relation to the permanent surroundings. All this may sound intricate and confusing, but fundamentals should be understood before attempting to create a personal artistic expression. A mere jumble of haphazardly placed rocks does not constitute a rock garden; it rather becomes an obtrusive rock pile and an unsightly development in the otherwise cozy surroundings of the home grounds. A rock garden, when well planned, can be made attractive in almost any location, whether in the front or back yard, with or without a slope.

On most home grounds, particularly in cities, where the land is level and the plot is small, a cactus garden must be frankly artificial. Such a rockery should be placed in some corner of the yard where it will not harshly interfere with the general outline of the landscaped grounds. This type of a garden should be made as natural in aspect as possible, inspiration being derived from rocks on natural hillsides. On the other hand, a rockery consisting of cactus plants only is a complete garden in itself and will not look out of place even in the center of the lawn. I have seen some excellent cacti beds in the front yards of Texas and Arizona homes.

Never build a rockery in the shade of trees, as desert cacti and the other succulents delight in full sunlight. An unshaded place usually can be found in a corner of the yard near the garage or the ash pit, or possibly in the curve of the border. The best rocks for a cactus rockery are those which are porous and moisture absorbing, such as the sandstone and limestone found in the Middle West. The honeycombed rock so eagerly sought for rock gardens because of its porous nature is admirable, but any kind of rock can be used, even boulders. The soil in a rockery for succulents should be of a light sandy consistency. As for the grouping of such plants, there is no set rule.

Planting cacti directly in the ground is not recommended in the colder climes where permanent planting is impossible, because there is danger of injuring the roots when digging them up for the winter removal indoors. It is better to leave them potted and to plunge the pots in the soil to within an inch of the rim. Gravel or limestone chat may be used as a ground cover to conceal the pot rims. Plants exposed to sunshine and rain during the summer months will do far better than those kept indoors. The beauty of a rockery of semitropical and tropical cacti can be increased by a permanent planting of some of our hardy succulents, such as the Prickly Pears, the native Sedums, Talinums, and others.

Where a rockery is not permissible, the plants can be placed outdoors by arranging a group against some sunny portion of the house, placing the tall ones in the back and graduating the rest down to the lowest in the front. This will be better for watering and even distribution of light. At any rate, it is always best to set the plants outdoors wherever possible —the desert kinds in full sun and the jungle types under trees or where partial shade is available. However, if you have no available yard space, a back or front porch is a good place for the plants. I built up a five-step wooden rack which I set against the wall of our back porch and placed the cacti on the tiers for a pleasing effect. There are many ingenious ways for growing cactus outdoors in the summer even in a small location. If there is a wooden fence, for instance, shelves can be added onto it without taking up space and potted plants set on the shelves. You'll be surprised how many plants can be accommodated there! If there is a shed, garage, or porch attached to your home with an accessible flat-topped roof, why not arrange the cacti there as a penthouse attraction.

CHAPTER V

# *PROPAGATION OF CACTI*

## FROM SEED

Have you ever tried growing Cacti from seed? To be sure, it requires patience—a lot of patience—but the effort will be rewarded many times over. To the hobbyist it is one of the cheapest means of obtaining a large collection of these strangely fascinating desert plants. Furthermore, it is surprising what a large and commendable number can be grown in the small space of an ordinary window of the average flat dweller.

Then, too, cacti that are grown from seed in the home will prove hardier and less liable to loss than most plants that have been transplanted from their desert environment and forced to adjust themselves in their new surroundings. Not that imported cacti from their natural habitats cannot be grown successfully; but these mature plants very frequently are received with unsightly injured spines, areoles, and other damaged organs that probably will cause their death. Those growers who have grown the plants from seed will be fortunate in possessing the long-lived varieties and getting their money's worth.

Among amateur plant lovers, the growing of cacti from seed has be-

# MATERIAL FOR SEED PROPAGATION

FIRMING SOIL
WITH TAMPER

PLACE GLASS
COVER OVER
SEED PAN

SOWING
SEED

GERMINATION

SIFTING THIN
LAYER OF SOIL
OVER THE SEEDS

TRANSPLANTING
SEEDLINGS INTO
INDIVIDUAL POTS

WATERING BY
IMMERSION

come a great fad, simply because no other group of plants offers such a wide variation in growth. Let me assure you, a more fascinating pastime cannot be indulged in than growing cacti from seed. A great thrill will be gotten from the day the seed is placed in the ground and shortly as it germinates into tiny ball-like bodies or spindly, cylindrical shapes until the day when the seedlings attain maturity and reward their benefactor with glorious bloom. In some species this does not take long, perhaps two or three years in the case of most Rebutias and such thimble-size cacti, but generally it will take much longer. A grower in Great Britain has proved that flowers can be obtained on *Mammillaria longiflora* within fourteen months of sowing the seed. There are others that will flower one year after seed sowing. Eriocereus and Selenicereus, both night-blooming genera, may require from five to seven years to attain blooming stage.

Those who are blessed with a patient temperament can acquire a notable collection of cactus plants in a few years by this method of propagation alone, but it is advisable not to depend on this mode entirely lest the slow growth of certain individuals cause a restraining effect on the culturist. Collections should be enlarged by the acquisition of a few specimen plants of flowering size, either through exchange of excess seedlings or by outright purchase, for in some instances it it not always possible to secure seeds of your most desirable species at opportune times, or again it is not profitable to grow others from seed when these plants can be bought very cheaply and conveniently from dealers, especially when the market is flooded with them.

Raising cacti from seed will not only produce a greater appreciation for most of these seemingly grotesque vegetable monstrosities, but the experiment will give many delightful moments the like of which cannot be described but must be experienced.

Now a word about seeds. Most cacti produce seed in abundance. For example, *Ferocactus Wislizenii,* the commonest and most widespread of our Southwestern barrel cacti, is one of the greatest seed producers in the cactus family. From eight to fifteen or more yellowish fruits crown the top of each plant, and each normal seed pod will yield approximately 1,600 seeds. The globular *Gymnocalycium Mihanovichii* has had 2,040 seeds in one berry by actual count, whereas the small, club-shaped fruits

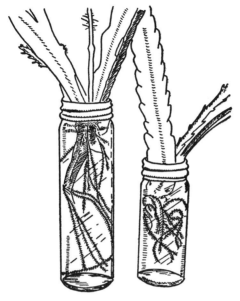

JUNGLE CACTI CAN BE ROOTED
IN WATER

SEEDLINGS SPROUTING
IN FRUIT OF FEROCACTUS

of Mammillarias average around 300 seeds per capsule. If nature would permit the germination of all these seeds, the waste places would become veritable jungles. However, but few ever sprout and develop into mature specimens because of the obstacles placed in their paths, such as unfavorable surroundings, absence of moisture, insect pests, foraging animals, etc. The amateur and professional plantsman will experience no difficulty in germinating seeds of cacti, whether he grows them in the greenhouse, in the sunroom, in the window of an ordinary home, or in flats and pans outdoors.

In most of the literature dealing with cacti there seems to be a universal understanding that fresh seed is of the utmost importance and that it must be sown as soon as possible. I, myself, have expressed the same opinion on several occasions in my lectures and articles, but additional experience over a long period of years has shown some doubt. True, there are a few species whose seed should be planted immediately, but the majority require a lapse of several months before being placed in the seed pan. I have noted in several instances that a much higher percentage of germination occurred when seeds were a year old than when sowed shortly after harvesting. Frequently, two- and three-year-old seed brought forth good results, the plants growing into fine specimens instead of supposed weaklings. Store packets marked "fresh seed" really are much older than they are advertised to be, but this need be no cause for alarm because they will germinate successfully. Should seed be harvested from home-grown plants it is advisable to remove all adhering pulp simply by rinsing in water and then drying out. If this is not done, fungus growth will make its appearance on the seed coat, which is detrimental to the germination process.

When I gather ripe seed pods of cacti, I usually cut open the fruit, squeeze out and spread the seed contents on a piece of stiff paper, and expose the seed to the sun for a few hours in order to dry out the mucilaginous substance surrounding each seed. After a thorough drying, the seeds can be easily brushed into an envelope and made ready for planting. In the case of less fleshy fruits, like those of Mammillarias which are thin-skinned, it is wise to dry out the capsules gradually and then store them until needed.

Cactus seeds can be planted anytime in the year if hothouse facilities are available, but in the average home the ideal time to sow is in late spring, that is, about the end of April or the beginning of May. The greatest calamity befalling early seed sowings is fluctuating temperature, a condition which is general in most homes at that time of the year. In the greenhouse, where more constant conditions prevail, such a risk can be greatly lessened. Successful seed planting can be carried on generally from April to the end of September, but during the hot summer months additional care must be exercised in not permitting seed pans to dry out. A uniform temperature of 70 degrees F. should be provided for most species, but 80 to 90 degrees F. will serve those from tropical regions to better advantage.

Light and frequent ventilation is just as important as warmth and moisture. In the home, seed pans should be placed in a window with a southern exposure so that sunlight will have a penetrating effect on the seed. Fresh air can be supplied by removing the glass cover from each seed pan, but only on days when the surrounding atmosphere is warm. If these four requisites are heeded, most cactus seed will germinate readily under house conditions.

Any low wooden, metal, or earthenware container can be utilized; but the ordinary porous seed pan, such as the growers use, is much more suitable. For smaller plantings, the regular three- or four-inch flower pot is commonly recommended. Cactus seed may also be sowed in flats or any other properly prepared seed beds. This small matter rests entirely upon the grower's fancy.

After choosing a suitable container, fill the bottom with a reasonable amount of the necessary drainage material in the form of broken crocks or coarse gravel. Upon this sift some prepared soil to within an inch of the top. Any good porous soil can be used, and almost every grower has his own formula, but the one recommended and easily prepared is composed of equal parts of well rotted leaf mold, screened sand, and ordinary garden loam. A small quantity of pulverized charcoal can also be added to this preparation. Beware of using soil that has a clay base, as it is too heavy and will not drain readily. If clay soil must be used, it will be advisable to use a soil conditioner, such as Krilium—one of the best on the market. The soil composition should be thoroughly mixed and screened through a quarter-inch mesh before being put into the seed pan. To insure a smoother surface, it is advisable to screen an additional layer—one inch deep—of like mixture through an eighth-inch mesh upon which the seeds are then placed. This last screening eliminates all fibrous and otherwise coarse ingredients in the soil which later harbor various minute fungoid growths that are injurious to the seed and seedling alike.

Before broadcasting seed in the pan, gently firm down the soil in the container with a circular wooden block or any such instrument to insure an even and smooth surface. When sowing seed it is best to segregate each genus. The finer seed can be scattered over the surface, but the larger should be laid uniformly in rows and care should be exercised to give each seed enough free space in which to develop. Finer seed should not be covered at all, but a sifting of soil or sand just sufficient to cover the larger seed is essential. Then a light covering of fine gravel is added. This serves as a protective blanket for any sudden drying out, as it aids in retaining moisture around the seeds and likewise insures support for the tiny plantlets after germination.

After all these sowing operations are performed, place the seed pan in a saucer filled with water, or in any other container, and permit the moisture to penetrate the soil from below. When the topsoil begins to show dampness, remove the seed pan from the saucer and empty the water. The length of time between such waterings will depend upon the conditions maintained around the seed pans as regards heat and ventilation. In the home these receptacles are likely to dry out quicker than in a greenhouse; so it will be necessary to water from below every fourth or fifth day. In the greenhouse, watering by this method will suffice for one week to ten days. Some cactus seed propagators prefer to water from the top, but unless a very fine, mist-like spray can be created, this method is not recommended for the beginner. Overhead spraying may cause the seed to float toward the edge of the pot and become bunched up.

When the seed pan has been moistened, place a glass cover over it and set in a well lighted window. Some seed will sprout within a week or a fortnight, whereas others may take several months. When germination has occurred, raise one side of the glass cover by inserting a matchstick under it to admit fresh air. Seedlings must be guarded against the burning rays of the sun, but after about a week or so the tiny plants may be exposed to strong light for short moments daily until they gradually become accustomed to it. Watering from below is preferable until the plants become sufficiently strong to withstand overhead spraying.

Early transplanting is to be avoided unless the tiny seedlings begin to crowd each other. The germinated seed may be allowed to grow for several weeks, perhaps months, in the original seed pan.

The process of transplanting requires great care, for the very soft and juicy cactus "babies" are tender and must be handled with caution lest they be accidentally squashed or injured. To prevent possible damage by finger pressure, it is wise that the novice use some sort of a device in handling the soft seedlings. An easily made contrivance is a small piece of wood, or better still a wooden plant label, with a one-half inch long, narrow slit at one end. With this simple instrument the tender plants are lifted up, after loosening the soil about them, and transplanted either into small flats or larger seed pans, using the same soil mixture as for the seeds.

The young plants should be spaced about an inch apart to allow space for development. When shifting the seedlings, care should be exercised not to injure the exceedingly fine and delicate rootlet that each plant possesses; and, for safety, do not apply water immediately after transplanting, but wait at least two days so that if any of the roots were damaged accidentally during the transferring process they will have sufficient time to heal over. It is also highly desirable to keep the plants in a shaded location for a few days before placing them in a sunny position.

The faster growing species may be transplanted as frequently as required. Frequent shifting of seedlings will not necessarily hasten growth. Certain species have a quicker rate of growth than others.

As to watering, there is really no set rule, but remember not to permit the soil to dry out completely, as this will prove very harmful, just as too much water is likewise injurious to the plants that do not dry out fast. The best method to follow is to water frequently but to use a very little amount each time.

There are but a few reliable seed dealers in this country, as well as abroad, who offer a wide selection. Back in the early thirties more seed dealers were in operation, particularly in Europe; but World War II depleted collections and seeds were harder to get. Even today, most nurserymen save their own seed for propagation purposes as there is a thriving trade in seedlings for dish gardens, bowls, etc. It is quite probable that seeds of a good many cacti will be limited for some time until more normal conditions prevail. Watch the various horticultural trade journals, particularly those that cater to cactophiles, for the names of seed dealers. A survey made recently reveals a few dealers from whom seeds of cacti can be procured.

Cactus and Craft Shop
Route 1
Middleboro, Massachusetts

Fritz Schwarz
Apartado 347
San Luis Potosi, S. L. P.
Mexico

Willi Wagner
Quinta Fernando Schmoll
Cadereyta de Montes, Qro.
Mexico

Harry Blossfeld (wholesale)
P. O. Box 2189
São Paulo, Brazil

H. Winter
Kakteen,
Frankfurt A.M- Fechenheim
Germany

W. T. Neale & Co., Ltd.
Franklin Road
Worthing
Sussex, England

Johnson Cactus Gardens
Paramount, California

Rocking Horse Cactus Gardens
2415 W. Glenrosa
Phoenix, Arizona

## FROM CUTTINGS

Many cacti produce numerous tiny plantlets along their stems. One of the best examples is the South American genus, Echinopsis, having long trumpet-like flowers, commonly called Easter Lily Cactus. Some of the species produce such an abundance of offsets that they literally cover the whole plant. These offsets or "pups" readily become detached from the mother plant and strike root when coming in contact with soil. Many a proud owner of an Echinopsis has supplied his neighborhood with starts from his plant. Oftentimes the offsets produce rootlets while still attached to the mother plant.

There are other cacti that exhibit offspring either at the top or bottom of the old plant, but some of these do not detach themselves as easily as do the Echinopsis; therefore, they must be cut off.

The cactus grower who possesses single plants and wishes to increase his stock of them can do it quickly by cuttings only. Don't be afraid to

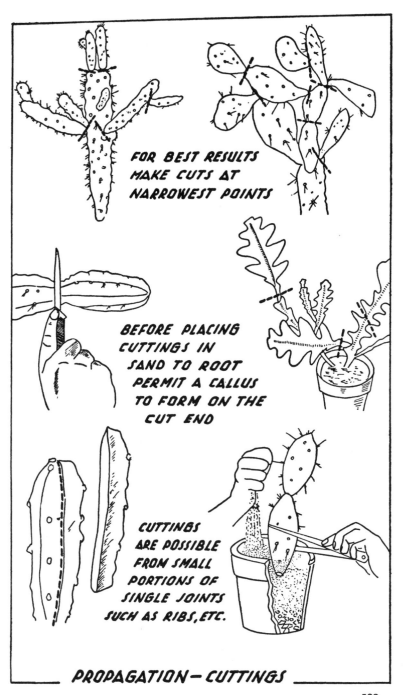

FOR BEST RESULTS
MAKE CUTS AT
NARROWEST POINTS

BEFORE PLACING
CUTTINGS IN
SAND TO ROOT
PERMIT A CALLUS
TO FORM ON THE
CUT END

CUTTINGS
ARE POSSIBLE
FROM SMALL
PORTIONS OF
SINGLE JOINTS
SUCH AS RIBS, ETC.

PROPAGATION — CUTTINGS

decapitate a plant. Although this procedure may seem drastic to some people and an occasional plant may be killed through carelessness, generally it will prove profitable. Once you've learned how to make cuttings, you will enjoy your success immensely, and you will always have a reserve of plants for trading, for grafting, or just for keeping in case the mother plant dies out.

The small cacti that produce a tuberous root, like the Ariocarpus, Lophophora, Aztekium, and Leuchtenbergia, should be cut off just below the head and the head grafted onto a good stock rather than rooted. The lower part of the tuber should not be discarded as it can, and often will, throw out new shoots which, when big enough, can be severed and carried on as cuttings. However, extreme care must be taken not to get water on the cut surface, as rot develops easily. Water by immersing the pot in a pan of water and, in this way no moisture will get directly on the decapitated plant. It might be worthwhile to put such a plant in a partly shaded location so that the cut surface will not dry out too rapidly, and even a glass cover over the pot after the cut surface has healed sufficiently will prove beneficial.

Almost any portion of a cactus stem can be cut off, treated, and induced to produce new growth. All cuttings with a large cut surface must be placed in a dry atmosphere for a few days in order for a callus to form over the wounded section. This is very important, because cuticle that is not healed properly will be subject to bacterial rot, which will quickly destroy the cutting. Cacti with small exposed surfaces, such as Aporocactus, Epiphyllum, Rhipsalis, Selenicereus, and the like, form a protective tissue in a few hours.

When taking or making cuttings from cacti, be sure to use a clean sharp knife or razor blade. If the stems are jointed, always cut at the base of a joint, because at the point of contact the cut will be smaller and therefore will heal faster. If a stem cutting must be taken elsewhere, this is permissible; but, since the cut surface will be larger, care must be exercised to allow a callus to form before the cutting can be placed in sand or sandy soil for rooting. Never be too hasty to place the cutting in the rooting medium unless well scarred over.

Although most cuttings may be placed directly in a mixture of sand and soil for convenience, pure sand or vermiculite seems to be a better

rooting medium. It is not necessary to place much of the cutting below
the rooting mixture. In fact, it is better to place all thick-stemmed varieties only on the sand surface and hold them in position, by means of
sticks, to prevent them from toppling over. Some cacti will produce a
vigorous root system in a short time, but ordinarily it will take longer
than two weeks. New shoots along the stem or the elongation of the
growing tip usually is an indication that the cutting is forming roots.
Water should not be applied to a cactus cutting until some sign of
growth appears, but always be cautious not to apply too much at one
time.

## BY GRAFTING

Perhaps it may be needless to explain what grafting really is, especially
to those who have already tried the experiment. Yet there are quite a
few cactus fanciers who indubitably have not the slightest idea what
this simple mode of plant propagation signifies, for what purposes it is
intended, and the results accruing from it. Many beginners discouragingly
look upon grafting as an art that can be successfully carried out only by
the advanced student. However, this is but a prevailing misconception
among novices, for truthfully there is no foundation to it. Grafting can
be accomplished by any person who possesses a reasonable amount of
common sense. Grafting not only is a very interesting phase of cactus
culture, but nowadays it is almost essential for each collector of these
bizarre plants who wishes to have the cacti looking their best at all times
or to enable the more delicate and rarer kinds to become productive in
the usually unfavorable environments of their adopted homes.

To be sure, grafting is an art; but, on the other hand, it is but a simple
process by which it is possible to unite two distinct plants and induce
them to function as one. In plain words, a sturdy grower is forced to
act as a support for a weaker member and to supply nourishment to it.
The two plants that are joined are commonly known as the stock and
the scion. The stock is a rooted plant upon which the scion will depend
for its existence; while the scion is a rootless cutting that is inserted
upon the stock. Care should always be taken that the stock be such that
it will sustain the graft for a long time. If it is weak or lacking in mois-

ture, the scion will not get enough food and will fare rather poorly, eventually drying up entirely.

By grafting it is possible to produce marvelous results in a relatively short time. By this means it is feasible to "step up" or accelerate the growth of grafted individuals by a year or more. Likewise it aids certain delicate and weak growing types to gain a firmer grip on life than they

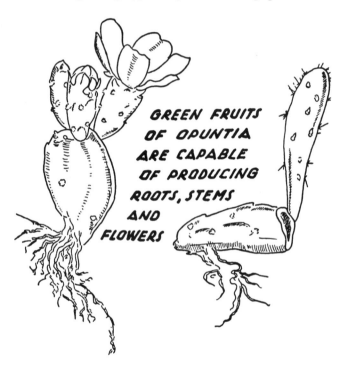

GREEN FRUITS OF OPUNTIA ARE CAPABLE OF PRODUCING ROOTS, STEMS AND FLOWERS

could if grown on their own root. By this method one is able to preserve those cactus varieties that are susceptible to a rot disease due to their parts coming in contact with a moistened soil.

Grafting also serves the purpose of propagating slow growing species more quickly. It aids tiny seedlings to attain maturity faster than if allowed to grow in the soil; saves such contaminated plants which, when cut to the healthy tissue, would be impossible to grow as a cutting because of the much reduced plant portion; insures a greater number of flowers; develops bushy and more decorative plants; and preserves abnormal forms, such as crests and monstrosities, which oftentimes are much harder to grow on their own root system and still harder to propagate by any means other than grafting. There are various other reasons for the fusion of cactus plants, but those enumerated cover all the chief purposes.

Even though the process of grafting is very simple, it is a good idea for the beginner to possess some knowledge relative to the plants involved and to the performance of the operation, so that this mode of cactus preservation and propagation will be successful.

Plants that are to be used as stocks must be in full growth—that is, healthy, full of sap, and owning a good root system. Of course, there are exceptions to this rule, as it is possible to graft some varieties with success on fresh Opuntia cuttings and certain Cerei and then place the grafted stocks in sand to root. However, this method is somewhat awkward and not advised for the amateur.

Grafting is best accomplished during the spring and summer months, preferably May to September, when the plants are growing well. Although successful grafts have been made at all times of the year, they are not recommended during the fall and winter months, as it will take a much longer period for the plants to unite and begin growth. Only when it becomes necessary to save injured or diseased plants during the cold months should grafting be resorted to in the unfavorable season.

There are three common methods for grafting cacti: the cleft, the flat, and the side. All thin-stemmed plants are suitable for cleft grafting, and the thick and globose types require a flat graft. A side graft can be used for either the thin or the thick species. Directions for all three of these operations are very simple.

*Cleft Graft.* In cleft grafting, cut back stock to a desired height, six to twelve inches preferably, and then make a slit at the top about an inch deep. The cut should never be much longer than the insert if a perfect union is to be attained. The stem of the scion is then cut on two sides to form a wedge and is inserted into the split of the stock. After firming the graft into the desired position, the scion is held in place by running a spine or two through the united portions and wrapping some string or raffia around the graft to prevent the slit from drawing apart. The wrapping cord should be taut enough to hold the scion in place and yet not so tight that it cuts into the stock. The use of wax is not required in cactus grafting.

*Flat Graft.* When using the flat graft, both scion and stock should be approximately the same width at the intended union. After selecting the two plants, make a smooth transverse cut on each specimen, and then place the scion on the severed stock, pressing the two flat surfaces firmly together. As a means of holding the scion, the use of two large-size rubber bands (or more, as the case warrants) is found highly efficacious. These should be placed gently over the top of the scion and run underneath the flowerpot, thus insuring tightness. Here, precaution should be taken so that the rubbers do not mash the graft or injure it in any way, especially on such soft-textured plants as the Pincushion or Nipple cacti (Mammillarias, Coryphanthas, etc.). The heavy textured Astrophytum, Ariocarpus, Echinopsis, Gymnocalycium, and others will stand much more pressure without any apparent injury than Mammillaria, Lophophora, Coryphantha, Rebutia, etc. In place of elastic bands, wrapping twine or string can be substituted. To prevent the cord from slipping, file or cut four equal grooves on the flowerpot rim as well as on the bottom and then run the string in the notches and over the plants to secure the graft in position. It will be a good idea to place some cotton or cloth over the scion where the string is apt to cut into the plant. Another method to hold the grafted plant in place is to take a piece of fairly flexible but stiff wire, bend it into the shape of the letter "U" and then, inverting it (so that the bent portion will come over the plant), anchor it into the soil. There are various other practical ways by which fresh grafts can be held in position, and only by experience will a definite method become suited to the individual's taste.

*Side Graft.* The side graft requires no special operation beyond slicing one side of both scion and stock and fastening the two joints in place. Slender plants, such as the Mistletoe Cactus and the Peanut Cactus, are usually used for this type of grafting.

When all grafting operations are completed, set the plants in a warm and shaded place so that the cut surfaces will not dry up too rapidly, thus preventing perfect unions. Water must be applied carefully for several days in order that no moisture will have a chance to gather on the cut parts. If a drop of water remains even for a short while there is a pos-

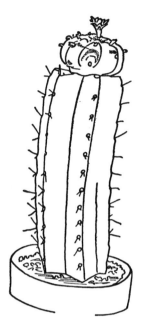

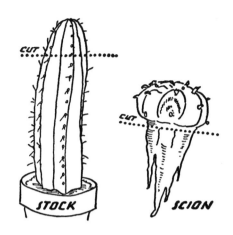

STOCK

SCION

CUT TOP OF STOCK AND BOTTOM OF
SCION. PLACE SCION ON TOP OF
STOCK AND HOLD IN POSITION
BY MEANS OF STRING OR RUBBER
BANDS.

## THE FLAT GRAFT

CUT SCION ON BOTH SIDES
TO FORM A WEDGE. INSERT
SCION INTO SLIT OF STOCK.
HOLD IN PLACE BY MEANS
OF SPINES. WRAP STRING
AROUND THE GRAFTED
PORTIONS.

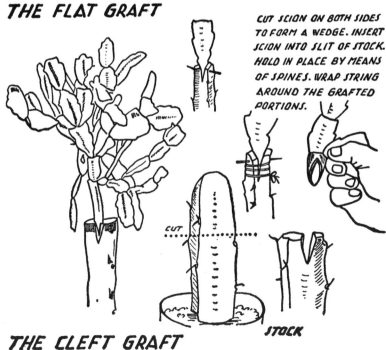

STOCK

## THE CLEFT GRAFT

115

sibility of rot setting in and eventually spoiling the grafting attempt. To prevent this accident and to guard against any possible fungus that might get a start on the fresh wounds (especially on stocks whose cut surface exceeds that of the scion), it is advisable to expose the newly made grafts to about thirty minutes of sunlight, so that a thin, membranous covering will form over the exposed fresh cuts.

Inspect all grafts occasionally to note whether union has formed properly. Sometimes it happens that, after about a lapse of one week, the stock will contract and produce a depression under the scion, eventually tearing the whole united growth apart. This may be due to several causes. Primarily the binding twine or other support may have been too loose to permit the two surfaces to weld together evenly and perhaps the surrounding air was too dry in addition, causing rapid evaporation from the cut portions. Then, too, the elastic bands, string, or wire supports may have been removed too soon. These props should not be removed for at least a month, unless they become too tight for the scion. Rather, leave the supports on a little longer than to withdraw them too soon.

Another precautionary measure to observe and one that will prove beneficial in averting "bad luck" with grafts, especially if such small globose and short-cylindric plants as Rebutia, Lobivia, and Frailea, are set upon Cereus stocks having prominent ribs protruding from the central axis, is to cut the ribs at a slight angle. This eliminates the hard outer skin and any spine clusters which would interfere in making a good union. When the scion is placed on top of the somewhat higher, flat center of the stock and held in place by elastics, there is no chance for the stock to push out the graft. If moisture should accidentally gather on the cut surface, it will run off readily. To some such a graft may look unsightly for the first few months, but eventually the graft will cover the slanting portions and completely surround them with its growth.

Perchance some information may here be desired about the different types of stocks; which ones are most acceptable for receiving grafts, where to get them, and how to manage a steady supply for reserve.

The best stocks are members of the Cereus group, especially those that produce sturdy, upright growths in relatively short times. Among the best is the genus Trichocereus, with several good species such as *Spachianus, lamprochlorus, pasacana, Schickendantzii, macrogonus, candicans,* and others. Most of these varieties can be grown readily from seed and some species will be ready for grafting purposes (but only to receive smaller scions) in about two years after germination. The Trichocereus stocks are exceedingly ideal for flat grafts because their stems, when cut, present a large almost evenly round surface upon which various pincushion types of cacti can be set with ease. The genus Cereus also comprises a goodly number of forms suitable for flat grafting. The better known varieties are *Dayami, validus, peruvianus,* and *jamacaru.* Upon these sturdy stocks it is advisable to graft cacti that have wide bases, as the Astrophytums, Lobivias, Lophophoras, Malacocarpus, Notocactus, Echinopsis, and also most of the Mammillarias.

The broadleaf cacti, known botanically as Epiphyllum, will likewise produce enormous growths on Cereus stocks, especially if *Cereus validus* is used. Numerous other Cerei can be utilized, such as Harrisia, Hylocereus, Lemaireocereus, Nyctocereus, Pachycereus, Selenicereus, and Myrtillocactus. In fact, there is no limit to the number of good species in this tribe that may be used to advantage as stocks.

The pendent cactus plants as the Rat-tail (Aporocactus), the Peanut (Chamaecereus), all Rhipsalis, and the slender growing Wilcoxia, Peniocereus, and others are usually cleft-grafted upon shortened stems of Hylocereus, Harrisia, and Selenicereus. The Christmas, Thanksgiving, and Lobster cacti (Schlumbergera and Zygocactus) with their hybrids, when grafted upon Pereskia stalks, will produce immense spreading umbrella-like heads of bright green joints which, at flowering time, become covered with a blanket of bright-colored blossoms. The slender branching Rhipsalis also seems to prefer Pereskia stems to any other.

The old-fashioned and well-beloved Christmas Cactus can also be grafted upon *Hylocereus undatus, Selenicereus pteranthus,* and even upon several Opuntias. The genus Opuntia contains but few species satisfactory for use as grafting stocks. Probably the best is *Opuntia subulata* with thick, almost cylindrical stems. This is ideal for Zygocactus, Schlumbergera, Rhipsalis, various pendulous types, and a number of the smaller Prickly Pear varieties. A few thickened, flat joints of Opuntias, especially the spineless or nearly spineless forms, are also utilized for grafting purposes, but not to a great extent. *Echinopsis Eyriesii* is probably the best of all stocks and is universally used for almost any type of cactus plant, whether a seedling or a large specimen. In European countries, this species, as well as all its congeners, is commonly used for safeguarding the rarer imports rather than risking them on their own roots.

It will pay the individual, who expects to do plenty of grafting in season, to prepare his stocks during the winter months so that the plants will be well rooted and ready when needed. As a rule, most of the afore-mentioned plants may be readily grown from slips; and, if any of the species are in the possession of the cactus collector, he should avail him-self of all the cuttings he can secure from such plants.

In earlier paragraphs of this chapter the reader is enlightened in the various ways of making cuttings and of increasing his supply from single plants. Whenever cutting away the upper portion of a Cereus to make way for the placement of the scion, it is recommended that enough be cut away so that the top piece can be used for a cutting rather than dis-carding it. In consideration, the severed segment must be at least two inches long for rooting purposes.

Another worthwhile tip may be of interest. After cutting off a scion, as of Lophophora, do not throw away the remaining portion of the lower or underground stem, but permit it to grow. Generally, this part tends to produce adventitious shoots, thereby allowing an alert cactophile to increase his stock twofold. Those who have not the opportunity to pro-duce grafting stocks from their own private plants are reminded that such rooted (as well as unrooted) cuttings can be easily secured from the nurseryman at nominal prices.

Sometimes certain stocks will have the tendency to produce suckers or offshoots either at the base or infrequently along the stem. When these make their appearance it is advisable to remove them immediately; other-wise the scions will be deprived of much nutrient matter, thus hindering the growth of the grafts. Pereskia stems and Echinopsis usually produce these suckers in abundance.

Grafting can be started in the early part of March and, even if these plants are not in full vegetative growth, they will outgrow those grafted in July and August.

After the grafting process is completed, no other care (except that already mentioned in the preceding paragraphs) is necessary. However, it will be practicable to transplant grafted plants about once a year to insure good soil conditions. A little liquid manure is beneficial in the growing season.

CHAPTER VI

# INTEREST IN CACTI

THERE ARE many cactus clubs scattered throughout the United States and in foreign countries throughout the world. Cactus fans in the United States wishing to join any particular group are referred to the following clubs which are affiliated with the national society with headquarters in California. For further information on any cactus club the reader is invited to write the author at the Missouri Botanical Garden, 2315 Tower Grove Avenue, St. Louis 10, Missouri.

## Cactus and Succulent Society of America, Inc.

This nation-wide organization was formed in January 1929 at Los Angeles, California. The Society launched its first copy of the *Cactus Journal* with the July 1929 issue; and the magazine, the most outstanding of its kind, has been published uninterruptedly ever since by Scott E. Haselton, able editor, at Pasadena. The publication encourages the amateur culturist of cacti and succulents, benefits the professional grower, and furnishes the reader with interesting, entertaining, and helpful material. Subscription to the magazine is $3.00 per year, which includes membership in the national society. Field trips and tours to private gardens are undertaken. Meetings, open to the public, are announced in the *Cactus Journal*. Biennial conventions are held in various cities where affiliate clubs are functioning. The fifth biennial cactus convention of the Society was held in Arcadia, California, in 1953.

## The Amateur Cactus Society of Chester

This southern Illinois society was organized on October 31, 1945. Meetings are held on the first Wednesday evening of each month at the home of the founder, Mrs. Ella Nipper. Dues are $1.00 per year. Projects include grafting, dish gardening, corsages, arrangements, growing plants from seed, window gardening, etc.

## Arizona Cactus and Native Flora Society

This society was formed to sponsor a Botanical Garden in Papago Park, near Phoenix, in 1937. It is not a cactus society in the accepted meaning of the term, but membership in the Society is actually membership in the Desert Botanical Garden with annual fees of $3.00 for active members. Members receive the *Saguaroland Bulletin* ten times a year which gives interesting reports on desert plants and keeps members in touch with Garden activities. A group of local people, known as "The Cactomaniacs," all of whom must be members of the Garden, meet on the first Tuesday of each month in the Webster Auditorium of the Garden, and a program of mutual help and information is followed by kodachromes of plants or localities. Meetings are held in the months from October to May only. Occasional field trips are undertaken. No dues other than membership in the Garden are required. The Garden was host to the third biennial convention of the Cactus and Succulent Society of America, Inc., in 1949.

## Cactus and Succulent Society of California

This society was organized in the early or middle thirties. Meetings are usually held on the second Sunday in each month, the meetings from October to April in Oakland, and from April to October at the various homes of members in the locality. Dues are $3.50 a year, which includes a subscription to the *Cactus Journal* published by the national society in Pasadena. Main project is an elaborate display staged each year at the Spring Garden Show in Oakland. Meetings consist of a lecture, travelogue, or the showing of slides, a plant table for members to bring interesting plants in bloom, etc. A good library is maintained as well as a greenhouse and yard in which to keep plants owned by the club and used in flower shows.

## Cactus and Succulent Society of San Antonio

This Texas club was organized on May 8, 1955. Meetings are held on the second Sunday of each month—the time and place decided at the previous meeting. Initial project started was the organization of a beginners' class in cultivation and identification of cactus and succulent plants. Field trips are sponsored in the fall season. It is the hope of this club to establish a public garden in San Antonio.

## Chicago Cactus Society

This club was organized in 1933 during the first year of the Chicago World's Fair. Meetings are held on the fourth Sunday of each month at 2:30 p.m. at the Garfield Park Recreation Center. Dues are $1.00 per year. The club carries on varied programs pertaining to cacti and the other succulents, discusses particular genera, and invites members to bring in specimens for study at the meetings. Occasionally slides of trips taken in cactus regions are shown. During the summer months, collections and gardens of the members are visited.

## Colorado Cactophiles

The club was organized in 1953. Meetings are held on the third Thursday of each month. Dues are $1.00 a year per family unit. Roll call is always answered with the scientific name of a cactus or succulent. There are either informal talks or occasionally a formal lecture, both illustrated with slides or movies. Club participates in the big All-Hobbies Show at the Denver City Auditorium. Services are offered to aid in the cactus and succulent section of the ambitious arboretum project being started at Denver's City Park.

### Denver Cactus and Succulent Society

The club was organized on October 1, 1938, with seven charter members. The purpose of the club is to promote the study and culture of succulent plant life. In summer, field trips are made to cactus localities, not so much to collect cacti as to observe them in their native habitat. Meetings are held on the last Friday night of each month. Dues are $1.00 a year. The society library consists of approximately fifty books on cacti and succulents. The club plant is *Coloradoa Mesa-Verdae*. In 1951 the Denver Society was host to the fourth biennial convention of the Cactus and Succulent Society of America, Inc.

### Des Moines Cactus and Succulent Society

This club was organized on October 17, 1938, at the home of Mrs. Virginia Wickliff. Membership dues are $1.00 per year. Meetings are held on the third Tuesday of each month. The club sponsored the Cactus and Succulent Garden in the Tropical Room of the City Greenhouse. Members of the Society serve as Hostesses during the annual Chrysanthemum Show and also make flower arrangements. Club flower is *Opuntia tortispina*.

### The Detroit Cactus and Succulent Society

This Michigan group of cactophiles was organized in 1943. Dues are $1.00 per year. Meetings are held every second Sunday of the month. One of the functions of the Society is to increase knowledge of cacti and succulents, and the members are asked to turn in reports at the meetings. Pilgrimages to the University of Michigan at Ann Arbor and to other places housing cacti and succulents are undertaken.

### El Paso Cactus and Rock Club

This club was organized on November 1, 1937, to study, promote, and encourage the cultivation of cacti and also to study rocks. Meetings are held on the fourth Tuesday of each month, the Hostess of the Month designating the meeting place and the telephone committee notifying the membership. Lectures are given at the meetings, and field trips are often undertaken. The club has a display at the Annual Flower Show. Dues are $3.00 per year. The club is host to the sixth biennial convention of the Cactus and Succulent Society of America, Inc., in 1955.

## The Epiphyllum Society of America

This specialized group was organized on May 5, 1940. Membership is spread throughout the world. The primary purpose of the organization is to clarify the names and descriptions of the numerous Epiphyllum hybrids which were in the trade and, until this club was founded, had been known as *Phyllocactus*. The dues are $2.00 per year. Meetings are held in January, March, May, July, September, and November. A mimeographed *Bulletin* is issued six to eight times a year. An annual Cut Flower Show of all forms of epiphytic cacti is staged in May in some part of Los Angeles County in California. In the fall a Picture Contest is held devoted to all forms of pictures with an Epiphyllum motif, and art objects and fabrics are on exhibit.

## Freeport Cactus Club

This north Illinois cactus club was organized on February 21, 1940. Meetings are held at the homes of the members and consist of lessons given by selected members who gather the information from articles written by professionals, followed by discussions. The club emphasizes the importance of visiting other members' collections for inspiration and new ideas. A cactus show is planned occasionally.

## Henry Shaw Cactus Society

This society was founded by me on July 12, 1942, with twelve charter members present. Regular meetings are held in the Museum Building at Missouri Botanical Garden, located at Cleveland and Tower Grove Avenue gate in St. Louis. Meetings take place on the second Sunday of each month at 2:30 p.m. Usually a featured speaker is on each program discussing some phase of cactus culture, often illustrated with kodachrome slides or movies. A plant of the month is featured and discussed, and an attendance prize is drawn. A mammoth fall cactus show is staged in the Flower House at Missouri Botanical Garden in September. The society publishes a nine-page mimeographed *Cactus Digest* which goes to members in all parts of this country and abroad. Dues are $1.50 for active members, $1.00 for subscribers, and $1.60 for foreign. Club flower is *Neobesseya missouriensis*. St. Louis was host to the first cactus convention of the Cactus and Succulent Society of America, Inc., in 1941.

### K. I. O. Cactus Club

This club was organized on July 1, 1937, at the home of Mr. and Mrs. Charles Cole in Cincinnati to take in members from Kentucky, Indiana, and Ohio. Dues are $1.00 per member. Meetings are held on the third Saturday of each month at 7:30 p.m., usually in the Irwin M. Krohn Conservatory, Eden Park, Cincinnati. Plants are sold and exchanged at meetings. Club was host to the second national convention of the Cactus and Succulent Society of America in 1947. The club was instrumental in getting a Cactus Wing erected on the Conservatories in Eden Park, which was completed and dedicated on November 4, 1939. Many books were presented by the club to the Lloyd Library and to the Garden Center. Placque and red-leaved Yucca were donated to the Desert Botanical Garden in Papago Park, Phoenix, Arizona, in memory of Mr. Irwin M. Krohn, late President of the Board of Park Commissioners, Cincinnati.

### Long Beach Cactus Club

This club was organized in March of 1933 by Mr. John Klenke for the purposes of promoting the general interest in cacti and the other succulents, in exchange of information on these plants, and to work for a public garden of the cacti and succulents. The club has planted and presented to the City of Long Beach, California, a large succulent garden in Recreation Park. The club takes pride in exhibiting in many of the garden shows and also for holding a very successful cactus show. The group meets primarily at the homes of members on the third Sunday of each month and the dues are only 50¢ per person a year.

### Los Angeles Cactus and Succulent Society

This club was originally organized in 1934 as the Southwest Cactus Growers. It changed the name to the present one in 1941. Meetings are held on the first Sunday of each month. Dues are $1.00 per year plus 50¢ for the *Cactus Chronicle,* a mimeographed monthly bulletin. There is a botanical talk at each meeting. Trips are undertaken to the gardens of members and to cactus localities in the State of California.

## Midwest Cactus and Succulent Society

This club was organized in August of 1936 with headquarters in Cleveland, Ohio. The membership is scattered through the surrounding territory and includes a number of enthusiastic fanciers of long standing, among them being John E. C. Rodgers, who is the author of "Cereusly Speaking," a popular column which has been appearing regularly in the *Cactus Journal* for many years. Meetings are held at the homes of members, or on occasion at the Cleveland Garden Center and the Cleveland City Greenhouses. A library of cacti and succulent literature has been assembled. Annual dues are $1.00 a person or $1.50 per couple.

## New Mexico Cactus and Succulent Society

This club was organized on November 6, 1954, with sixteen persons present. The second formal meeting was held on January 20, 1955, at which time dues were decided upon in the amount of $1.00 per family of husband and wife, or one person. Meetings are held in Albuquerque and Santa Fe.

## Oklahoma Cactus and Succulent Society

The club was organized on November 14, 1934. Meetings are held at the homes of various members. Activities are confined to the study of cactus and succulent plants. The club cooperates with local flower show in Oklahoma City. Dues are $1.00 per year for a member. At present the club is seeking permission to plant a complete garden of Oklahoma cacti on the rocky points along the Turner Turnpike.

## Philadelphia Cactus and Succulent Society

This club was organized on November 15, 1942. Meetings are held at the Morris Arboretum in the months of February, April, June, October,

and December. Flowering plants are brought to the meetings to be discussed. Dues are $1.00 per year.

*Sarasota Succulent Society*

This club was organized in the fall of 1950 with ten charter members
for the purpose of studying the culture of succulents under local conditions, their correct nomenclature, their use in landscape design and as
specimen plants, and also to aid in civic projects involving this specialized
study. A rock garden was started on ground loaned by Mr. W. G. Sparkman at the corner of Myrtle and Coconut Avenues in Sarasota, Florida,
and negotiations are under way to purchase the plot. The garden is open
to the public on visitors' days and the members cooperatively care for
the plants. A slat house was also built. A library is maintained and an
exhibition is put on at the local flower show. At first, meetings were held
in private homes, but now a room is set aside in the Sparkman residence
where careful study and work in the experimental garden is undertaken.
Each member is invited to write a paper or prepare a program for one
of the meetings, which are held on the first Friday of each month at
2:30 p.m. Dues for active members are $2.00 a year; and for associate
members, $5.00 a year.

## FOREIGN ENGLISH-SPEAKING CLUBS

*Cactus and Succulent Society of Great Britain*

This society was founded by E. Shurly, Esq., in November, 1931, at the
St. Bride Institute in the City of London. During World War II the activities of the society were suspended for the duration, but in 1945 the
club was reorganized with fifty members attending the first meeting. At
present, six hundred members are on the roster. The Society publishes
a *Cactus Journal,* which was started in 1932. It is a quarterly edited by
Mr. Shurly. The activities of the club center around the Journal. The
Society has a very extensive free distribution of seed to its members, some
thousands of packets going out every year.

*National Cactus and Succulent Society*

This society was organized on August 23, 1945, when the Messrs. A. Baynes, F. Ives, V. W. Kane, and H. M. Roan discussed at great length the possibilities of forming a club to bring together cactus enthusiasts in Great Britain. The men met at the home of Mr. H. M. Roan, and it was decided to call the new organization the Yorkshire Cactus Society. However, in the latter half of 1946 the name was changed to the present one because the society became national in scope. The society has grown to be the largest of its kind in Europe. Branch clubs have been established in all parts of the British Isles, each one holding its meetings on special days. There are twenty-five branches operating at present. A quarterly *Cactus and Succulent Journal* is published. Subscription for Ordinary Members is £1; for Junior Members 10/6; and for Associate Members 5/-.

*The London Cactus Club*

This club was organized to cater to the beginner with a few plants on a window sill as well as to the enthusiast with a collection filling a greenhouse. Meetings are held once a month at the Royal Horticultural Hall, where lectures are given by leading authorities and fellow-members. Each member receives *The Cactulent,* official monthly journal of the club which contains articles on all aspects of the hobby. A comprehensive library for the use of members is maintained. Facilities are given for the acquisition of plants and equipment at reasonable prices. The dues are low, 10s. per annum full, 15s. joint man and wife, 5s. juniors under eighteen years.

*Cactus and Succulent Society of New Zealand, Inc.*

This society was organized in 1947 and since has grown to be the largest cactus club in the Southern Hemisphere. Eleven branch clubs are established throughout the Dominion, and each branch is an entirely self-contained unit, with its own officers. The *New Zealand Cactus and Succulent Journal* is the official organ of the society with dues fixed at 12/6 for adults, 7/6 for juniors, and 5s. for associates. Members resident in

New Zealand may borrow from the society's library by paying postage and a few pence reading fee.

### Cactus and Succulent Society of Australia

I haven't been able to ascertain when this society was founded, but it must have been in the early forties and then lagged until it was revived in 1947. The following year, *The Spine,* official quarterly organ, was launched as an ambitious project. Members bring plants for competition to the monthly meetings. Books from the society's library are available for the use of country and interstate members. Membership is 10/– per annum per person, or 15/– per annum for husband and wife, and 2/6 for juniors.

# BIBLIOGRAPHY

## Cactus Reading for Pleasure and Profit

ARMER, LAURA ADAMS. *Cactus*. 102 pp. Frederick A. Stokes Company, New York. 1934. This little volume contains fifty full page line drawings by Sidney Armer of cacti and a few of their close companions that grow in the Great American Desert. In many instances, the drawings give the parts—spine cluster or flower—of the cactus, so that identification can readily be made. Opposite each illustration is a page of popular as well as botanical matter about the particular plant.

BAXTER, EDGAR M. *California Cactus*. 100 pp., 85 illus. and full color frontispiece. Abbey San Encino Press, Los Angeles, California. 1935. The only complete book on the native cacti of California. Thirty-nine species are described, including two new ones. The author has personally visited and photographed each of the species in their native habitat. A glossary of common names is valuable for local identification.

BENSON, LYMAN. *The Cacti of Arizona*. 134 pp., illustrated in color, black and white, and line drawings. University of Arizona, Tucson. 1940. This is a paper-bound, semipopular book for the identification of Arizona's cacti. Subject matter is outlined in an orderly manner, and keys are provided for determination of the scientific or popular name of any cactus. Each plant is described in considerable detail. Distributional maps are provided for sixty of the most important plants. A second edition was brought out in 1950 to include the changes, rearrangement of species, and revisions of classification as well as additional data upon the characteristics and distribution of species and varieties.

BERTRAND, A. AND A. GUILLAUMIN. *Cacti*. 94 pp., 51 photographs, and 8 natural color plates. Crosby Lockwood & Son, Limited, London. 1952. This is a lavishly illustrated small book, translated from the French, in which the authors have tried to give sound advice on culture. After explaining the natural conditions in which cacti grow, they go on to show the particular needs of each variety of near parentage.

BOISSEVAIN, CHARLES H. AND CAROL DAVIDSON. *Colorado Cacti.* 73 pp., illustrated with 42 halftones, one color plate, and numerous line drawings. Abbey Garden Press, Pasadena, California. 1940. This is an illustrated guide describing all of the native Colorado cacti and imparting a better knowledge of the truly hardy species suitable for outdoor culture in districts subject to severe winters.

BONKER, FRANCES AND JOHN JAMES THORNBER. *The Sage of the Desert.* 106 pp., 8 illus. The Stratford Company, Boston. 1930. This little book deals with some of the weird fantastic growths of the American Desert in a popular way by presenting certain simple facts of structure and design, environment, distribution, etc.

BORG, PROF. J. *Cacti.* 420 pp., 93 halftone illus. Macmillan & Company, Ltd., London. 1937. This is a gardener's handbook for the identification and cultivation of cacti. After a few introductory chapters of a general character conveying elementary knowledge on the cultivation, as well as cactus structure, a general classification is given with concise but full descriptions of the genera of Cactaceae and most of the species in cultivation, along with their varieties. A second edition was published in 1951 to include three hundred additional species.

BRITTON, N. L. AND J. N. ROSE. *The Cactaceae.* Four volumes, 1048 pp., profusely illustrated with black-and-white photographs and color plates, as well as line drawings. The Carnegie Institution of Washington. 1919-1923. This is the first comprehensive treatise on the Cactus family in the English language, which has come to be known as the "American Cactus Bible." More than twelve hundred species are described in detail and there are Keys to all the important groups. The Britton and Rose system of nomenclature serves as the basis for most of the cactus monographs of later authors; however, changes and revisions are necessary because of extensive research and new discoveries. The Cactus and Succulent Society of America reprinted *The Cactaceae* in 1937.

CARLSON, RAYMOND. *The Flowering Cactus.* 96 pp., 115 photographs, 81 in brilliant color. McGraw-Hill Book Co., Inc. 1954. This is the most colorful book on cacti published to date. The photographs were furnished by R. C. and Claire Meyer Proctor, who have chosen the most outstanding ones from their files. The Proctors, not only topnotch photographers but authorities on cactus plants, also supplied the technical data. George M. Avey did the excellent sketches which will help the reader to understand these plants, and Raymond Carlson edited the entire contents. This book will be cherished for its beautifully impressive color pictures.

CRAIG, ROBERT T. *The Mammillaria Handbook*. 390 pp., 307 halftones. Abbey Garden Press, Pasadena. 1945. The Mammillaria section of the Cactaceae has interested more collectors than any other genus. In this monograph, the author brings up-to-date all the available information on this very interesting group of plants. The main body of the book contains detailed descriptions of 238 species. Twenty-eight other species are proposed and another hundred are briefly described. Associated genera, like Dolichothele and Bartschella, are also included.

DAY, HARRY A. *Flowers of the Desert*. 168 pp., 4 plates. Methuen & Co., Ltd., London. 1938. This is a small book, telling in simple language how to go about the cultivation of cacti and the other succulents. The author has assembled the various genera and species in more or less botanical relationship but, as he states, "in loose and incomplete manner." The first half of the book (82 pp.) is devoted to cacti and is an attempt to help the reader to grow cacti in the hope of obtaining floral display.

HASELTON, SCOTT E. *Cacti for the Amateur*. 160 pp., illustrated with many halftones, line drawings and a color plate of 110 species. Abbey Garden Press, Pasadena, California. 1938. In this book the author tries to answer thousands of questions on the care and culture of cacti and also endeavors to show in pictures and text that cacti can be successfully grown in city apartments, in mountain cabins, desert estates, etc. The author is the editor of the *Cactus Journal* and owner of the Abbey Garden Press, which has an enviable reputation in the publishing field.

HASELTON, SCOTT E. *Epiphyllum Handbook*. 222 pp., illustrated, indexed. Abbey Garden Press, Pasadena. 1946. The author presents a most thorough and meticulous study of the genus Epiphyllum, covering the natural habitat, history, best practices for growing healthy plants, varieties, etc. It is generously illustrated with numerous black-and-white photos and drawings, and many color plates. It is the most complete work on the particular subject.

HIGGINS, ETHEL BAILEY. *Our Native Cacti*. 170 pp., illustrated. A. T. De La Mare Co. New York. 1931. In classification the author follows Britton and Rose in their Cactaceae. Bits of romance, the common names, snatches of history in our Southwest, economic uses, decorative values are included in the book.

HIGGINS, VERA. *The Study of Cacti*. 164 pp., 12 illus. Blandford Press, Ltd., London. 1933. This small handbook describes the Britton and Rose genera of cacti, gives hints on methods of cultivation, and contains an important chapter on nomenclature.

Houghton, Dr. Arthur D. *The Cactus Book.* 147 pp., 18 illus. The Macmillan Company, New York. 1930. The author has endeavored to give a readable review of the cactus family. A "conspectus of species" takes up 30 pages and lists in a unique and helpful manner the native habitat of about a thousand species, the amount of sun or shade required, the most desirable soil, moisture requirements, hardiness, habit of growth, and color of flowers.

Lamb, E. *Flowering Your Cacti.* 56 pp., illustrated with 21 photos. W. T. Neale & Co., Ltd., Worthing, England. 1943. This little book deals with the cactus and cactus-like succulents, their general culture, and the success the author has had in producing flowers. The booklet is designed to give those interested in cacti not merely a few hints on culture, but a useful "Reference Calendar" which can be applied to suit your own particular plants.

Lawson, H. C. *Book of Cacti for the Amateur Collector.* 36 pp., over 200 illus. Lawson Cactus Gardens, San Antonio, Texas. 1935. In the body of the book are pages illustrating nearly two hundred and fifty species of cacti native of the United States and Mexico. Following are notes briefly describing the species illustrated and numerous others. The book should familiarize the amateur with the different types of cacti.

Manning, Reg. *What Kinda Cactus Izzat?* 108 pp. J. J. Augustin, New York. 1941. In this cartoon book the author has dished out a great deal of scientific information about cacti in the acceptable form of amusing cartoons which are held together with a light running account of the desert plants one encounters in the southwestern "cactus belt." If you want a book with which you can sit down with pleasure and get many a chuckle, get this one. An entertaining, amusing, and informative book.

Marshall, W. Taylor. *Arizona's Cactuses.* 111 pp., 64 illustrations, and several line drawings. Desert Botanical Garden of Arizona, Phoenix. 1950. A small book describing the native Arizona cacti written in nontechnical language. Descriptions are adequate and understandable. Definitions of specific names are given as well as their pronunciation.

Marshall, W. Taylor and Thor Methven Bock. *Cactaceae.* 227 pp., 166 halftones, 31 plates of brush and ink drawings. Abbey Garden Press, Pasadena. 1941. This volume describes all of the acceptable new genera and species since Britton & Rose's monumental work on the family, as well as the changes in classifications necessitated by recent discoveries. The book is of inestimable value to the collector, grower, and student of the Cactaceae.

Matschat, Cecile Hulse. *Mexican Plants for American Gardens.* 270 pp., illus. Houghton Mifflin Company, Boston and New York. 1935. The author spent seven years with her engineer husband in Mexico and had numerous opportunities to visit gardens and become acquainted with plants. The chapter on cacti is titled "Dwellers in the Sun" and consists of forty-five pages.

NEALE, W. T. *Cactus and Other Succulents.* 200 pp., 160 illustrations. Meeching Rise Nurseries, Newhaven, Sussex, England. The first 30 pages are devoted to introductory material, propagation, and cultural information. The next 120 pages comprise a list of cacti and other succulents which are grown or stocked by the author in his nursery. The readable descriptions of the various genera and species are designed to interest the beginner and amateur. This work is better classified as a "book-catalogue."

ROAN, H. M. *Cactus and Other Succulent Plants—A Primary.* In cooperation with C. R. Hancock and M. Clague-Taylor. 55 pp., 110 illustrations and line drawings. The National Cactus and Succulent Society. 1948. A handy booklet intended for the novice, giving cultural hints on cactus plants as well as other succulents. A second edition was necessary in 1949 which gives additional information; the book is simple and nontechnical.

SCHULZ, ELLEN D. *Cactus Culture.* 157 pp., Orange Judd Publishing Co. New York. 1932. A readable little volume intended to instruct the amateur in the elements of the art of growing cacti, with some excursions into the field of other succulents. The instructions are simple and adequate and the photographs for the most part well selected.

SCHULZ, ELLEN D. AND ROBERT RUNYON. *Texas Cacti.* 181 pp., 63 photographs. Texas Academy of Science, San Antonio. 1930. A popular and scientific account of the cacti native of Texas. A bibliography, a glossary, and a list of common and local names is included.

SHREVE, FORREST. *The Cactus and Its Home.* 195 pp., 55 photographs. The Williams & Wilkins Company, Baltimore. 1931. This book is not only helpful to those who are primarily interested in the cactus, but is intended to stimulate the study of natural history of our arid and semi-arid states. The author describes what the cactus is, how it is constructed, its names, its tribes and families, how it may be cultivated both outdoors, when climatic conditions are favorable, and indoors where they may be simulated.

VAN LAREN, A. J. *Cactus.* Translated from the Dutch by E. J. Labarre. 150 natural color illustrations. Abbey San Encino Press, Los Angeles. A worthy volume in a limited edition, using the Britton and Rose nomenclature. The illustrations are excellent and will enable the reader to determine his plants. Large type is used which will be welcomed by those whose eyes are no longer young.

WATSON, W. *Cactus Culture for Amateurs.* 246 pp., illustrated with woodcuts. L. Upcott Gill, London. 1889. This possibly is the first popular book on cactus written in the English language. Watson was the caretaker of the large cactus collection housed in Kew Gardens in England, and therefore could write with authority. The descriptions of the plants are simple and complete, and the cultural directions ample. Many of the names listed in the book are obsolete now.

WERDERMANN, DR. E. *Brazil and Its Columnar Cacti.* 122 pp., 89 illustrations, 1 map. Abbey Garden Press, Pasadena. 1942. This book, originally published in German in 1933, was translated into English by Robert W. Kelly. It gives an interesting account of the author's trip through the little known desert wilderness of eastern Brazil. Descriptions of the inhabitants, a keen sense of humor and the detailed geographical accounts make this book worth reading. The last 36 pages occupy keys to the columnar cacti with accompanying descriptions and are clear and based on plant characteristics wherever possible.

# INDEX

Boldface type indicates illustrations.